Special Talents, Special Needs

5

Special Talents, Special Needs
Drama for People with Learning Disabilities

Ian McCurrach and Barbara Darnley

Jessica Kingsley Publishers
London and Philadelphia

The right of Ian McCurrach and Barbara Darnley to be identified as authors of this work
has been asserted by them in accordance with the Copyright, Designs and Patents Act
1988.
First published in the United Kingdom in 1999 by
Jessica Kingsley Publishers Ltd,
116 Pentonville Road,
London N1 9JB, England
and
325 Chestnut Street,
Philadelphia
PA 19106, USA

Second impression 2000

www.jkp.com

© Copyright 1999 Ian McCurrach and Barbara Darnley

Library of Congress Cataloging in Publication Data
Ian McCurrach, Ian.
Special talents, special needs : drama for people with learning disabilities /
Ian McCurrach and Barbara Darnley.
p.   cm.
Includes bibliographical references.
ISBN 1 85302 561 5 (pbk. : alk. paper)
1. Learning disabled--Education--Handbooks, manuals, etc.
2. Drama in education--Handbooks, manuals, etc. 3. Special education--Handbooks,
manuals, etc.   I. Darnley, Barbara.
II. Title.
LC4704.5.M23 1999
371.9--dc21   98-49772
CIP

British Library Cataloguing in Publication Data
McCurrach, Ian
Special talents, special needs : drama for people with learning disabilities
1. Theatre – Study and teaching 2. Learning disabled – Education
I. Title II. Darnley, Barbara
792'.087

ISBN 1 85302 561 5

Printed and Bound in Great Britain by
Athenaeum Press, Gateshead, Tyne and Wear

Contents

Part I: An Introduction to Creative Expression Through Drama

Part II: Progressing and Developing the Work: Exploring Theatre Skills

Acknowledgements

The authors would like to thank the Strathcona Theatre Company, especialy Ann Cleary; Professor Sheila Hollins for the opportunities at St George's Medical School; all the staff and students past and present of the Special Needs department at Kingsway College, London; everyone at Paddington Arts; the staff and students at Westminster Physical Disabilities Unit; Pat Place and Artsreach; SHAPE; Keith Barlow; and their families for all their support. The authors also give special thanks to their students at Kingsway for providing the pictures for the book.

Preface

Special Talents, Special Needs is a handbook for teachers and facilitators working with learning disabled people who are interested in creative expression through drama. The authors draw from their work over fifteen years in a variety of theatrical contexts. Ian as Joint Artistic Director of Strathcona Theatre Company – Europe's leading professional company of actors with a learning disability – has run workshops with many different groups of learning disabled students. Barbara, as an actress, also runs numerous dynamic drama workshops and residencies. In 1989, when we first started working in the field of drama for people with learning disabilities, our search for appropriate source material quickly drew a blank. We had our own expertise as actors gained from experiences at university, drama school and work with countless professional directors from which to draw inspiration to lead workshops. Ian also has valuable experience from his time working through the SHAPE[1] network. Ten years down the line, we now feel appropriately equipped to pass on some of the experiences and techniques we have learned and developed and sincerely hope that this may help others starting out in this very rewarding field. Our book offers no form of direct therapy for people with learning disabilities. But work over recent years with the Strathcona actors and other drama groups has clearly demonstrated that work of this kind not only increases communication skills, but also promotes independence, self-esteem and well-being. We are not drama therapists and therefore we have not written this book from a therapeutic perspective. But it goes without saying that the value of the work to the students is manifest. Most students increase in self-confidence, develop better communication and

---

1   Shape is an organisation which co-ordinates and funds artists to work with disabled people in the community.

social skills, and improve their ability to work within a group dynamic. Our main aims are these:

- to help unlock the creativity and imaginative skills that are in everyone
- to create a stimulating and safe environment for enjoyable creative exploration
- to facilitate individuals to explore beyond their habitual boundaries.
- to involve other sections of the community in the creative achievements of learning disabled people.

HOW TO USE THIS BOOK

The book is divided into three main parts. The parts roughly correspond to the timetable of terms in a further education setting. The body of work is progressive and the supposition is that a core group of students will follow through to the end of the course, possibly to a final performance or showing of work. **Part I** provides an introduction to creative expression through drama. It is divided into ten sessions, the title of each indicating an individual focus of work. Every session includes a physical and vocal warm-up and develops from the previous workshop. At the end of each session there is a checklist of skills learned. **Part II** is a progression and development of **Part I** and explores Theatre Skills. The student is introduced to some of the crafts of acting over individually focused sessions, leading towards the idea of a final showing of work or performance using a theme. **Part III** covers the rehearsal period working towards a final performance or showing of work. We have also included detailed **lists of exercises** and improvisations in each part, so that someone running a less structured course can dip in and out of the book for inspiration and ideas, to fit in with the needs of their particular group. For those of you thinking big and contemplating taking your work to a wider audience such as other colleges or day centres, we have included some do's and don'ts of touring. *Special Talents, Special Needs* is aimed at drama students, actors and directors running drama sessions for people with learning disabilities, special needs teachers, keyworkers and day centre staff, youth workers, arts outreach workers and so forth. Another area of work is creating a dramatic and sensory experience for people with profound and multiple disabilities and we hope some people may find our notes on this subject useful. We are sure our book will help others leading drama groups to stimulate and liberate students' imagination and creative self-expression.

Introduction

CHECKLIST OF POINTS TO CONSIDER BEFORE YOU BEGIN YOUR SESSIONS

Who are your students?

1. As actors – Have your students chosen to come to your session, or is it something they have been timetabled to attend? If you have not personally selected the students by 'auditioning' at, say, an open workshop, it is important to find out what their expectation of a drama session is, and if they have had any previous drama experience.

2. As people – What will your students be like? We have learned it is probably better not to be given too much detailed information from a third party – carer, previous tutor, for example, as this may colour your personal reactions in some way – but you do need to know if there are any individual physical or behavioural problems that may affect the group's work as a whole.

Carers

Don't forget that some students may be accompanied by carers. Make them feel welcome and important – this almost always ensures that they will join in and help everyone enjoy the session. Carers are usually family members or support workers employed by the local authority. Remember, carers are there to support their clients and to support you; they are not there to judge your work. Do not feel inhibited by their presence, even though, at this stage, they will know their clients better than you – good carers should always be ready to try something new.

Sometimes, unfortunately, you may come across a support worker who is not willing to join in or has a negative attitude to the work. You must have a chat with them and find out why this situation has arisen, and if there is anything you can do to help. If the problem persists, particularly if you feel the client is being inhibited in some way by this attitude, you must take the matter further, probably by then speaking to the client's keyworker.

Assessing the space

Is it accessible to people with varying mobility? Are there toilets and changing facilities nearby? Are refreshment facilities available? Is it large enough and appropriate for the work you intend to undertake? Is it large enough to divide the group into two or three separate units? Do you know where the fire exits are? Is there a First Aid Box? Indeed, it's a good idea for you to have taken a first aid course in case of emergencies. Do you know how to adjust heating, lighting, ventilation? Is there a telephone? Who is in charge of the building? Do you feel comfortable with the space?

Using the above questions as a basic guide, make sure that you are happy with the space before meeting your group of new students.

Tea break

How long is the session? How many times a week will you meet? We suggest initially a two hour session, once a week. It may be appropriate when leading up to performance to increase this to twice a week. Assuming the session is two hours in length, a twenty minute tea break should be appropriate half way through. Tea breaks can be a good opportunity for social skills and, if there is a canteen, money handling, but remember they always take longer than you think!

Registers

If you are running your session for a Local Education Authority you will be expected to keep a register. In any case, it is a good idea to keep a record of attendance for yourself, which will be essential for evaluating students' progress. And of course a register becomes a vital tool in the event of emergency evacuation or fire drill.

Before your students arrive

Make sure you are in the room before your students. Bear in mind it is notoriously difficult to start a session on time. Students may come from a variety of places, for example, group home, day centre and so forth, and so are often reliant on local authority transport, which varies in its punctuality.

YOU ARE NOW READY TO WELCOME YOUR STUDENTS

First arrivals

As the group may take some time to assemble, you may need to delay the official start of the session until everyone has arrived. Your ground rules (see below) can include a mutually agreed 'waiting time', say twenty minutes, before you begin your session. This time can be spent, as appropriate, for example, chatting about previous sessions, talking about how the students' week has been, and simple warm-up games.

Ground rules

The ground rules should be established fairly early on, although not necessarily during the first session. Below are some suggestions:

1. Punctuality.

2. Commitment to attending the group and working with each other.

3. Mutual respect. Caring for the group. This includes no verbal and physical abuse, for example, swearing, hitting, unwelcome physicality of any kind.

4. Listening to you and to each other.

5. Personal hygiene and the wearing of appropriate clothing and footwear.

6 Toilet breaks – try to impress on everyone the need to leave the room only before the session begins or in the tea break. Some people disguise their nervousness of the new situation by continually wanting to leave the room.

7. Maintaining the above rules – devising a strategy such as 'Red Card' time-outs for any kind of disruptive behaviour, and 'Yellow Card' warnings for persistent personal lateness or non-attendance.

Welcoming your students and assessing students' abilities

As your new students are just that, new to you, you cannot possibly create in advance a rigid session plan before you've met them individually. However, as a general rule, it is best to have a session plan bursting with ideas, all of which can be jettisoned if the mood of the group suggests something different that day! You'll find yourself thinking on your feet.

Warm-ups are a very good way to gauge, and indeed change the apparent mood of the group.

ENDING THE SESSION

It is a good idea to end each session with the same structured ritual, so that everyone knows the session has ended and feels a sense of unity and completion. Something as simple as calling everyone back into the circle and giving time and space to recap and evaluate what has been achieved, and taking a few moments to give group or individual encouragement is often what's needed. Perhaps also to discuss what will happen next time, though you may well find that in some cases this information is not retained. Some people find it appropriate to begin the session with a lighting of a candle and end it with blowing it out. Others find a song a good rousing or soothing way to end. Then again you may feel a few minutes relaxation on the floor to peaceful music rounds things off for you, or perhaps a rousing Haka or cheer may be more appropriate for your group.

Whatever you decide, it's a good idea to finish a few minutes short of your official time as inevitably someone's transport will be early or someone else needs to leave promptly and it is good for everyone to leave on equal terms and not feel that they have missed out on something.

PART I

An Introduction to Creative Expression Through Drama

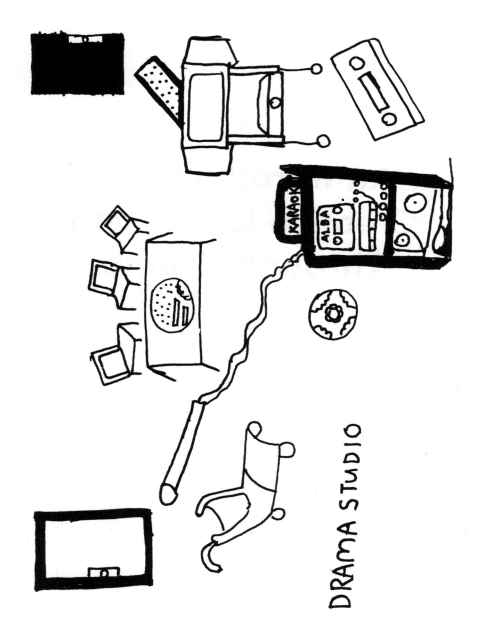

DRAMA STUDIO

Session 1: Getting to Know You

INTRODUCTION

As each student arrives make sure you introduce yourself and, where appropriate, shake hands. Once all students have assembled you are ready to start. It is important to explain at the beginning how the session is likely to progress. This should be done in a relaxed informal way so that no one feels pressured to perform. An overall view of the term/series of workshops should also be given. It is vital to say that students should not be afraid to try out new things as you are there to help them. They must at all times feel comfortable. Don't forget to add that everyone is there to have a good time and to enjoy themselves.

WARM-UP

In this first session the emphasis will be on getting to know everyone and learning names. In future sessions we will suggest physical and vocal warm-ups appropriate to the content of each session. As a general rule these will also incorporate something from the previous session, so that a body of familiar work is built up through repetition.

Perhaps it would be good to start the whole session, even before beginning to learn names, by gathering the group into a circle, establishing a quiet, anticipatory mood, and teaching them the *neutral* position. Feet slightly apart, knees slightly relaxed ('easy knees'), weight on both feet, arms by the side, head up eyes open and alert. From here they should feel ready to work.

EXERCISES/GAMES

1. Bathtime for Barbara

Students in a circle. Start with an introduction, for example 'My name is Barbara. This is a game to find out everybody's name. I'm going to think of an object or action that begins with the same letter as my name: B for Barbara. Bathtime for Barbara. When having a bath you have to wash yourself all over like this (demonstrate). I'd like you all to copy the action and repeat the phrase: Bathtime for Barbara.'

Move on to the person on your left who says their name, chooses an action, everyone repeats it, *and* your name/action.

Tools	None
Rules	Play the game in groups of four going round the circle. When you reach the person on your right, tell the whole group that after they've heard this last name they must go right back round the circle repeating everyone's name and action, finishing with an extremely loud *'Bathtime for Barbara!'*

2. Alphabet Queue

Ask students to line up alphabetically, using first names.

Tools	None
Rules	This must be done in silence. Previous games should have established names.
Variations	(a) Once in the queue ask students to imagine what they are waiting for; for example, a bus, doctor's surgery, to see a pop star. What position could the body be in to express each individual's attitude to the wait? Can they express it (i) vocally (ii) in mime?
	(b) Each individual could think of an adjective to describe their attitude to waiting that begins with the same letter as their name, for example Bored Barbara, Ill Ian, and could mime how that feels within the queue.

3. Body Words

In groups, ask students to spell out a short name using their bodies to form letters. They can either do this as upright words, or lying on the ground to be 'read' from above. Each letter can be made by one, two or three people. The exercise shows students how their bodies can be used to form inanimate objects.

Tools   None

Rules   Make sure the names can be read from left to right. Each group should be able to remember their body positions in the word long enough to read the other group's word.

TEA BREAK

4. Name That Ball

A well-known game, useful for initial introductions and, as here, as a deceptively simple eye contact exercise.

Tools   A large soft ball. A cushion, or even a plastic bag stuffed with something soft and readily available like a jumper can be used if some students have particular difficulty catching things. The ball is thrown from person to person.

Rules   Eye contact must be made *before* the ball is thrown. The thrower must then say the name of the catcher *loudly*.

Variations The ball becomes imaginary. It becomes heavy, very light, a hot potato, a sticky sponge, a precious jewel.

5. Getting to Know You

Students in a circle to listen to your instructions. 'In a moment I am going to ask you to move around the room. When I say *stop* I want you to stop and listen to a question. I'll give you a minute to think of your answer. When I say *go* I want you to move around the room greeting as many people as you can like this (demonstrate a hand clasp, or similar) and tell each new person the answer to my question.'

Tools   Suggested questions:

- What is your favourite TV programme?
- What is your favourite food?
- What are you frightened of?
- Who would you most like to be, if you weren't you?
- What are you good at?

Rules   When you have finished your questions ask the students to reform the circle. Who can remember anything about someone that they met? For example, 'I met Ian and he is afraid of spiders!'

6. Making a Machine

In groups, ask the students to make an object with moving parts, creating a machine.

Tools   None, unless really necessary.

Rules   Break the object into its component parts, for example a fruit machine could be broken down as follows:

One person

- as the operating handle
- another with their mouth open – could be used as slot to take coin
- a third as one of the discs spinning round
- a fourth as the next spinning disc
- a fifth as the next spinning disc
- a sixth as the tray which pours out the money.

In the above example it might be fun to use a coin and to have several being thrown out of the tray at the bottom, and to have someone operating the machine.

Ask students to make the noise the object would make with their voices.

7. Relaxation Journey

Any students in wheelchairs should be asked to sit as comfortably as possible with their eyes closed. Ask the other students to lie down on the floor if it is reasonably clean, or preferably on mats. If possible everyone should be flat on their backs. Ask them to close their eyes and remain silent concentrating on their breathing, while you take them on a relaxation journey/story to end the session. At the end, perhaps ask them to gently come up to a sitting position and ask them how they have felt about their first session, and give them any necessary information about next time.

Skills checklist

✓ Have you learned the names? Have the students been able to remember some names? Next session you can take the opportunity to recap names in the warm-up and in further games.

✓ How have the students inter-reacted? You may have got some inkling of who works well together, or conversely who it would be best to separate – keep an eye on this during the next session.

✓ Have students been able to give each other time and space to think of ideas, or have some people got impatient? Emphasise that everyone is here to enjoy themselves and must be allowed to work at their own pace – there will be opportunities for everyone to take 'centre stage' at various points during the course.

✓ Have they listened to instructions and replies? Talk about the need to listen and be quiet at the appropriate time.

✓ How relaxed did they seem by the end of the session? With themselves, each other and you? Look back at our notes in the introduction on *Ending the Session* and think about possible ritualised ways of conducting future sessions.

✓ Has *Name That Ball* revealed any particular co-ordination skills or problems?

✓ What has *Bathtime for Barbara* revealed about imagination?

Session 2: Communication

INTRODUCTION

Theatre is communication. The performer and the audience must want to share emotions, ideas and information for a theatrical event to take place. To this end, actors must communicate with each other as well as with the audience. Actors and performers communicate in three different ways; physically with their bodies, verbally using speech and sound, and emotionally – which is generally a combination of both.

In this session we will concentrate on general exercises which are designed to help students communicate with each other and reach out to an audience.

WARM-UP

Physical warm-up

Students in a circle. As this is their first physical warm-up, lead the group through warming up their bodies from top to toe. For example, stretching, circling, swinging, balancing movements, possibly repeated eight times for each different part of the body. Music can be useful.

Vocal warm-up

Students in a circle. Let's see if any names have been retained from last time. One at a time the students go into the centre of the circle and announce their name. The whole group repeats the name. The student in the centre then becomes a 'conductor', and controls the volume of name repetition.

Different ways of controlling the volume can be explored. For example, the student can use simple hand signals like the conductor of an orchestra or can use the whole body in various different ways – reaching up to the ceiling could indicate 'get louder', crouching down on the floor could indicate 'get softer'. Students can take it in turns in the centre to develop different volume control signals.

Before beginning this session's exercises it is a good idea to talk about communicating. A good way of defining communication for students is to describe it as the way we give messages to each other and express emotions – and that we communicate with our bodies as well as with our voices.

EXERCISES/GAMES

1. Presenting Self With Action

Students at one end of room. Ask each student, one at a time, to go to the far end of the room. When they get there they must turn round to face the others, the audience, then come forward and at a given point half-way down the room they must present themselves to the audience, with an action. For example, hands outstretched, bowing, clapping, jumping, etc.

Tools	The presentation spot can be marked with a taped X or a physical object such as a jumper or a scarf.
Rules	Each person must come forward confidently, at the very least lifting eyes from the floor and making some eye contact with the audience.
Variation	You could suggest abstract actions, for example spiky, curvy, etc. or suggest various incarnations, for example an animal, a clown, an acrobat, etc. Encourage the students to make the action as large as possible.

2. Hello, My Name Is...

As above but this time the students must announce themselves saying, 'Hello, my name is...'

Tools	None, although it can be effective to use a door and ask the student outside to first knock and for the others to say 'ready'.
Rules	Again make sure the student makes eye contact with the audience from the presentation spot. Encourage a loud voice.
Variations	The students can come forward in small groups, two's or three's and present themselves with a small 'routine' which

they can work out. This is particularly useful if individuals are reluctant to express themselves on their own.

Another variation is to change the exercise into an end game with the students finding different ways of presenting a 'Goodbye' routine. This could be a simple farewell wave or a complicated improvisation.

3. Circle One Word Association

Students sitting in a circle. Ask them to go round and say their names, one after the other, to get them used to sequence speaking. Once they have done this ask them to say in sequence the first thing that comes into their head. It can be quite interesting to see what comes out.

Tools	If students are having problems choosing a random word or anything at all, it can be useful to pass round an object at the same time – the object takes the focus away from having to vocalise an idea.
Rules	Make sure students are relaxed and let them know that it does not matter what they say. There is no right or wrong.
Variations	If this is going really well try and see if you can go round saying a well-known rhyme, for example a nursery rhyme 'Happy Birthday' saying one word or phrase at a time.

4. Giant Gestures

Ask the group to think about how they tell each other things with their bodies and without using speech. Make a list of movements that mean different things.   For example, shrug, nodding yes, headshaking no, waving, smiling, crying, hitch-hike thumb.

Students in a circle. Each person takes it in turn to come into centre of circle and gesture. The rest of the group follows.

Tools	None.
Rules	There must be no talking.
Variations	Students in pairs having conversation without speech using gesture only.

For example

Hello

Drink?

No thanks

Suit yourself

I'm late

What for?

I'm going to post a letter

Bye, then

Or one student coming into centre of circle gesturing. The others have to guess what he/she is 'saying'.

TEA BREAK

5. Knives and Forks

Language and gesture are common currency built up over time. Motorist's hand signals are the language of traffic, shortening a horse's reins and squeezing with your legs tells a horse to go faster. We can experiment with changing the language of commands. This is quite a hard game which is appropriate to some groups and not others.

The students stand at one end of room facing forward. Call out instructions from the front – knives, forks, cups and saucers.
When the call is:

Knives – students take a step left

Forks – students take a step right

Cups – students take one step forward

Saucers – students take one step back.

Tools   None.

Rules   Spend time making sure that everyone understands the instructions.

If played altogether this game can get very noisy so impress on students that concentration is essential.

Variations   (a) Students work in pairs with one person calling the instructions, and then swapping over.

(b) As a race, with one caller.

(c) Instruction codes can be invented and demonstrated by different groups.

6. Do You Like Your Neighbour?

Students in a circle with one person in centre. There must be one less chair than people. The object of the game is for the person in the centre to sit on one of the chairs in the circle. To do this they ask 'Do you like your neighbour?'

Before starting this game it is a good idea to ask each person in the circle to name their neighbours – the person on each side of them. Frequent reinforcing of names is always valuable.

It is easiest to describe this game using real names.

Nick (student in centre): 'Do you like your neighbours, Tim?'

Tim: 'Yes, I like my neighbours.'

If the answer is yes, nothing happens and Nick chooses someone else.

Nick: 'Do you like your neighbours, Ali?'

Ali: 'No. I don't like Rommel, and I don't like Peter.'

Nick: 'Who would you like?'

Ali: 'I'd like Susan and Robert.'

When Ali says 'move', Rommel and Peter have to swap places with Susan and Robert. Meanwhile Nick must try to get a chair. Nick can only take Robert's or Susan's chair as Ali did not want Nick as his neighbour.

Tools   None.

Rules   No one must move until their name is called. The person being questioned must remember not to move.

Variations   A further complication can be the 'All Change' rule. In the above sequence Tim could say he does not want anyone as his neighbour – 'I don't want anyone' – in which case everyone else gets up and stands behind their chairs (Nick stands behind Tim's chair). When Tim says 'move' everyone moves clockwise round the outside of the circle. When Tim says 'stop' everyone must rush to a seat. The person who does not get a seat is the next person in the middle.

7. Zip, Zap, Boing

Students in a circle. This is an exercise in which a movement is passed around the circle.

ZIP

Begin by holding your arms out with hands together in a V shape (with palms together). Pass the V shape to the person on your left, saying ZIP. The next person does the same until ZIP has gone all the way round the circle. Keep practising this until everyone has got the idea. Try passing the ZIP shape round the circle in the other direction.

ZAP

ZAP changes the sequence. ZAP someone by stretching arms out parallel and say ZAP plus the person's name, for example, ZAP JOHN. It is important that the name is said so that everyone knows who you are ZAPPING.

BOING

To BOING you push your hips out as if you are pushing something away which returns the action to the previous person.

Tools   None.

Rules   You cannot ZAP your neighbours (the people immediately on either side of you) but you can ZAP anyone else. Each person can only BOING a maximum of three times in a row.

 Again this game gets very lively so students must really concentrate.

Variations It's a knockout! This game can be played with a time element – if people take more than five seconds to decide what to do, they are out. If they do something wrong – ZIP with a ZAP action etc., then they are also out.

Skills checklist

✓ Have you communicated the rules of the games successfully? Take your time; you will learn to pace yourself and your teaching methods according to the group's needs – don't be afraid to give each exercise the time the group needs to explore it. Remember it is the quality of what you do that matters, not the number of exercises per session.

✓ Have students been looking at each other when they have been communicating? Introduce the students to the importance of eye contact as you will be looking at this further in the next session.

✓ In *Presenting Self With Action* have students remembered the target spot, raised their eyes to their audience and used a loud enough voice? Each student will have different levels of progress on this one – comment and praise individual achievement.

✓ In *Word Association* have they been able not to worry about the meaning of their word and speak spontaneously? This may be an overly verbal exercise for some students, but nevertheless they may enjoy being part of the circle and may take inspiration from other students' offering suggestions for their contribution. On the other hand, guard against one more able student, enthusiastically speaking for everyone.

Skills checklist continued

✓ Have they been able to associate *Giant Gestures* with everyday methods of communication? Has a hearing impaired student been able to share any sign language or Makaton?

✓ In *Knives and Forks* have they understood that language is just an agreed form of communication and that other words can be used to mean the same thing? Have you talked about this in relation to foreign languages?

✓ *Do You Like Your Neighbour?* and *Zip, Zap, Boing* should finally have established names, and encouraged choice making.

Session 3: Eye Contact

INTRODUCTION

What makes us feel included in a conversation? How do we recognise when someone is speaking to us? How do we feel when someone speaks to us without looking at us? What does it say about a person when they talk or try to communicate while looking at the floor?

Eye contact is a very potent 'tool' in most communication, and on stage, where the detail of everyday life is heightened, it becomes especially important. Actors need to look at each other in order to share the moment on stage convincingly with each other and the audience. They need to raise their eyes from the stage and 'greet' and 'challenge' the audience, making them feel part of the creative experience.

WARM-UP

Physical warm-up

Shake out, make your body as big as possible, make your body as small as possible, stretches.

Eyes, keeping your head still and your eyes open; look up, look down, look right, look left. Screw your face up tightly; opposite, open mouth and wide eyes. Make animal gestures; be as big as a lion, as small as a mouse. Concentrate on the face, make a Cheshire cat; big smiles. Make a horse; blow through the nose and push lips forward and neigh.

Ask the students if they remember any of the communication gestures they discovered during the previous session. Take suggestions. Choose about four, for example, shrug, hitch-hike thumb, nod and wave. Combine them into a repetitive sequence and introduce music playing in the background. Choose music with different moods, and see how this affects the movement. Point out that the students were able to create this sequence and stay in time with each other because they were using their eyes.

Vocal warm-up

Big yawns; making as much as noise possible, introduce big and then bigger stretches to match the sound.

Students in a circle in the neutral position. Ask them where their voices come from? Talk about the power of sound coming from the centre, 'tummy', rather than purely from the throat. Ask them to place hand on diaphragm and breathe in and out regularly, then add the sound HAH. Increase this to HAH, HAH. HAH, HAH, HAH and so on aiming for ten to finish. (Detailed and concentrated vocal control builds throughout the sessions.) From this, keeping hand on diaphragm try to repeat the word and sound H, H, HELLO. Repeat, elongating the E and the O sounds in the word.

Before beginning this session's exercises it is essential to talk through the idea that eye contact is an important form of communication – see Introduction.

EXERCISES/GAMES

1. Hello, How Are You?

Everyone must greet each other while walking around the room. See how many verbal and physical variations on saying HELLO students can find.

Tools   None.

Rules   Each person must look into each other's eyes as they greet each other. No one must be left out.

2. The Eye of the Circle

Students in a circle. Choose someone to begin. Let's call this person Number One. Number One chooses someone else in the circle to stare at. Let's call this person Number Two. When Number One has caught Number Two's attention using eye contact only, they walk towards each other across the circle, meet in the centre and swap places. Number Two then chooses someone else and so on.

Tools   None.

Rules   Eye contact must be maintained until they meet in the middle. If it wavers badly they must both begin again. Silence and concentration must be maintained throughout.

 Students waiting in a circle can lose concentration and focus. You can prevent this by asking for their help in deciding whether the eye contact has been held successfully. Also insist that everyone waits in the neutral position ready for action!

Variations   Upon meeting in the middle of the circle students can invent a greeting. This variation is also the basis of other exercises – swapping vocal sounds, actions, rhythms etc., and changing them.

3. Is There Something In My Eye? (Brief Encounter!)

Has a friend ever asked you to look and see if they have something in their eye which is making it sore? Have you looked at people's eyes? Do you know what colour your friends' eyes are? Walk around the room taking care to stare deeply into the eyes of all the other students. If you can, tell them something about their eyes. It could be simply 'blue', or 'You have brown eyes', or something more imaginative, 'can I help you take that dust out of your eye?' 'You wear glasses'.

Tools   None.

Rules   Each student must make eye contact with everyone else. Then come back into a circle and see what has been found out about all the eyes in the room.

 Some people are reluctant to raise their eyes and heads from the ground. Discourage students from physical contact around the face, some may find such contact uncomfortable.

4. Friends Across the Sea

Students in as large a circle as possible. Ask everyone to imagine that they are on their own individual 'island'. One student goes in the middle and tries to get a message to someone. He/she spins round slowly in the middle and stops facing someone. When eye contact is made he/she can convey the message vocally, with megaphone, or with the scarves.

Tools   None, but could employ a cardboard megaphone or scarves to use as 'semaphore'.

Rules   Students in the circle must focus on the message sender all the time. The message cannot be sent until eye contact is made.

Variations   Group or individuals decide why they are on their island. What is each island like? Each student can send a different message, ranging from a simple *'HELP'* to a complicated rescue plan or even an order for a pizza! Those with limited vocal skills will find the semaphore scarves helpful for attracting attention and communicating.

 TEA BREAK

5. Band Leader

There are many different names for this game, but *Band Leader* was the name given to it by a particular student called Lionel with whom we were working. Lionel had problems making himself understood but was always trying to explain the rules of his favourite game, asking the group to play it. Finally after about three sessions we suddenly realised that the game he was explaining was a game that we knew, called *Who's Leading the Group*. It was such an achievement for Lionel to explain something quite complicated that the group decided that in future it would be known as *Band Leader!*

Students in a circle. One student is chosen/volunteers to leave the room. The others elect a Band Leader who begins an action which everyone must mirror, or follow. The leader must move slowly and change the action at will. This is a good exercise for increasing confidence and encouraging leadership and creative initiative. The student outside is called back, goes into the centre of the circle and tries to work out who is initiating the action – who is the Band Leader.

Tools   None.

Rules   Everyone must try to disguise the fact that they are looking at the Band Leader. Ask people to look at the person opposite them in the circle. You can play a stricter version whereby only one guess is allowed. If a wrong guess is made as to who is the Band Leader, the student is 'out'.

Variations   Isn't it obvious? Musical instruments! The Band Leader could take us through the whole orchestra!

6. Mirror Pairs

Students pair off and stand/sit opposite each other. Number One and Number Two. Number Ones are the leaders and begin a movement. It is best to suggest they start with small movements. Eye contact should be maintained throughout as Number Two mirrors all Number One's actions. Swap over. Movements will generally grow in complexity.

Tools   None.

Rules   Pairs should focus on the eyes, rather than the movement.

It is not a competition. Leaders enjoying their own actions can take off into a world of their own and leave their partner behind. Stress that chosen actions should suit both students.

Variations   If it's an exceptionally large class, in a smallish room, you can line the pairs up in two columns so that there are two people in the middle with their backs to each other. After a certain amount of time working in the first pairing you can ask the middle line to turn to face each other and invite the outside lines to get together – almost instant new pairings!

Give the pairs an emotion with which to colour their movements, for example, sad, happy, angry, frightened.

The emotional variation very often becomes vocal. Stress that it is a silent exercise, if that's what you need for the moment, or let the sounds come out and see where they lead. Some people find 'following' very difficult – wanting to 'lead' all the time. Try such pairings with facial movements – copying smiles and frowns can be successful.

7. Monster Murder

This is a game that can be great fun, as well as being a testing eye contact exercise. Because of the hilarity it can cause, it's probably best kept for the end of a session.

Tools   None, although a monster 'hat' could be transferred each time the Monster changes.

Students in a large circle. One student goes into middle – the Monster – and stretches out his/her arms in a classic 'Frankenstein' pose. The Monster chooses a 'victim' in the circle and advances towards them, staring at them all the time. If the Monster reaches them he/she will pretend to kill them and they swap over, the victim becoming the new Monster. To save him/herself the victim must find a 'saviour' by staring at someone else in the circle, silently asking for help. When the saviour notices that they are being stared at by the victim, they must call out the victim's name which saves and releases the victim. The Monster must then choose another victim to go after and so on.

Rules   Everyone in the circle must concentrate and focus on the Monster and each other so that they are prepared and ready for action.

 Be prepared for potential over-excitement.

Skills checklist

✓ Have some gazes been shifted from the floor? The smallest change in habitual patterns should be celebrated.

✓ Have some students maintained focus better with some students than with others? It is important to encourage successful pairings. At this point in the course, find out if there are any personal issues of fear or aggression to deal with. Similarly, discourage inappropriate couplings where there could be feelings of a sexual nature developing. Talk about the need to work well as friends in the class. If people want to explore personal relationships they need to do so outside of group time.

✓ Has the general level of concentration been raised? The group should be getting more used to working with you by now and developing an awareness of expectations and further explorations. Do not be put off by students talking fondly about previous drama tutors they may have worked with, and telling you how good they were! Learning disabled people often find it hard to let go, clinging to relationships they have made, particularly with authority figures and often find change challenging. You can be sure they will be remembering you as fondly at the end of the year!

✓ In *Band Leader* have students been able to lead and develop their own patterns of movement? Some student will always repeat the same actions – encourage further exploration.

✓ In *Mirror Pairs* have students been able to stick with each other, or has concentration drifted into their individual movements, or even into copying or being distracted by another pair? Asking individual pairs to demonstrate can focus both their attention and the group's.

✓ How is the group working together? Has respect for each other been maintained? In future sessions it may be interesting to explore pairings that have not worked well initially, reminding students of the need to be friends in the class.

Session 4: Concentration

INTRODUCTION

It takes a huge amount of concentration for any actor to perform a piece of work, and concentration is tiring. Some learning disabled actors find focusing on a task much easier than others, so clear explanations, patience and repetition are always of paramount importance in tackling any game, or indeed rehearsal.

It is important to stress that everyone should try to listen and concentrate all the time, even if the immediate focus is on an individual for a moment. This will help that individual to concentrate better on the task in hand and create a good working environment, where everyone can benefit from everyone else's notes. This leads to good habits in performance. We have all, sadly, been to the theatre and seen the eyes or smile of an actor waver, and destroy the credibility of a theatrical moment.

WARM-UP

Physical warm-up

Remind students of the game *Band Leader*. This time suggest that they pair up and go through their own series of exercises by mirroring each other and changing the leader when it seems appropriate. Or you can call out *'change'* if some people are getting stuck.

Vocal warm-up

A development of *Band Leader* is for each student to choose their favourite musical instrument. What sounds do they make? Try to re-create them vocally. 'Play' them individually and then put them all together to create a continuous sequence of sounds. Choose a 'conductor' or take the role yourself and make the sounds louder, softer, faster, slower.

Vowels – Students in a circle. Brainstorm the vowel sounds – who knows them? Teach them using the fingers of one hand to count them off. Make sure everyone is opening their mouth as wide as possible for each one. Teach them the 'Two finger drop' (mouth should be open at least the width of two fingers placed vertically in the mouth). Everyone repeats together the vowel sounds 'A E I O U' using fingers to count off as explained. Then see if students can do this on their own.

EXERCISES/GAMES

1. The Keeper of the Keys

One student sits on a chair or the floor, blindfolded, or with eyes shut, and a large bunch of keys in front of him/her. Two or three students are chosen to try to creep up and snatch the keys away before the Keeper can pick them up.

Tools   Large bunch of keys, or anything which makes a noise when moved. Blindfold.

Rules   Game should be played in silence. Before the game starts you should ensure that the Keeper can reach the keys when blindfolded – everyone has a different stretch. The Keeper is not allowed to keep his/her hand poised over the keys – both hands should be on his/her knees.

2. Crossing the River

Divide the students into two lines or 'teams' – Team A and Team B – facing each other with a good distance between the lines.

The aim of the exercise is to try to get as many people to cross over to your team as possible. The winning team is the one which has everyone in it! A volunteer from Team A has to call out, for example,

> 'You can only cross the river if you… are wearing tracksuit bottoms.'

> Everyone wearing tracksuit bottoms in Team B must cross over and join Team A.

> Someone on Team B then responds:

> 'You can only cross the river if you… have brown hair.'

Everyone with brown hair must cross from Team A to join Team B.

This sequence repeats itself, alternating from Team A to Team B until there is a winning Team, i.e. until everyone is on the same side of the river!

Tools   None – although a piece of cloth, or string, or two chairs at either end could represent the river.

Rules   Students must listen to the calls and think about what is being said. Encourage close observation and ask students to really think about the things that people have in common, which will mean maximum movement.

3. What are you Doing? or Liar!

This is a game which introduces mime and improvisation skills, and calls upon students to perform one activity whilst saying that they are doing something else – hence the name!

Students in a large circle. One player enters the circle and begins an action, for example, brushing his/her teeth. The next person in the circle enters the space and asks 'What are you doing?' The first player must think of another action and name it, whilst continuing to perform the original one, for example, 'I'm typing a letter'. The second player must then begin the second action, i.e. typing a letter. Once the second person begins typing a letter, the first person stops brushing his/her teeth and joins in with typing a letter. A third person joins and asks the second person 'What are you doing?' and is told another lie, for example, 'I'm digging the garden'. The third person then begins to dig the garden and so on.

Tools   None.

Rules   Students must make sure they are miming one action whilst saying they are doing something completely different or else they are out!

Variations   If students are finding it hard to concentrate progressing the entire group into the circle, then the game can be simply played with two at a time. Player One mimes one action, Player Two enters and questions what they are doing. After Player One joins in the mime suggested by Player Two, they swap over so that Player One asks Player Two what they are doing and they do something different. Once they have swapped over, Player One sits out and Player Three enters and follows the sequence until everyone has had a turn.

TEA BREAK

4. Grandmother's Footsteps

An old favourite, but one that really does test concentration.

'Grandmother' is chosen. She stands at one end of the room with her back to the other students. Whilst her back is turned students must advance towards her. The first to reach her and touch her shoulder becomes the next 'Grandmother'.

Tools   None.

Rules   Grandmother can turn round at any time. If she sees anyone moving they must go back to the beginning and start again.

     No giggling! Any sound is also a reason for returning to the start.

Variation   What's the Time Mr Wolf? A well known children's game.

5. Numbers into a Circle

A hard exercise which seems simple!

Students in a circle, possibly with eyes closed. The object of the exercise is to count to 10 or 20, without pre-agreeing who is to say which number. Students must listen for a silence into which they drop each number.

Tools   None

Rules   If two or more people speak at the same time you must begin counting again from the beginning.

6. Newspaper Islands and Sharks

Large sheets of paper or about 4 sheets of newspaper are laid together to form islands in the room – 'the sea'. Students move around the room until you call SHARK ATTACK whereupon the students must hurry onto the safety of an island. On the ALL CLEAR they begin to move around the room again, and you reduce the size of the islands progressively until only tiny islands with a lot of people balancing precariously are left.

Tools   Paper, and possible taped music to play in between shark attacks.

Rules   No parts of the body must touch the floor when on the islands. If this happens the player is out.

Variations A volunteer student can become a shark. When SHARK ATTACK is called the shark can catch anyone not completely on an island. Once caught, students join in and become sharks – possibly joining hands and becoming a 'Man-eating Shark' or 'Moby Dick'.

Skills checklist

✓ Have students been able to concentrate on the various tasks in some quite lively games? For example, In *Grandmother's Footsteps* have they been able to stay still and quiet? Also in *Keeper of the Keys*?

✓ Have they taken direction and returned to the beginning without a fuss when spotted moving? Some students can get hysterically giggly over this and you may need to partner them to encourage concentration. If a student becomes obstructive and refuses to return to the beginning when spotted moving, end the game unless the student agrees to comply with the rules.

✓ Has *Grandmother* been able to observe movement? Has *Grandmother* been able to assert herself enough to send people back to the beginning? Some students playing *Grandmother* may benefit from your help, or the assistance of a more able student.

Skills checklist continued

✓ In *Crossing the River* have students been able to identify common denominators? And use powers of observation and description? If students find this exercise challenging, break it down and work with one student at a time, identifying clothing, hair colour, etc. that the teams have in common.

✓ In *Liar* have they been able to copy an action? What level of imagination has been displayed in the choice of action? Some students find it impossible to do an action and say they are doing another. You may find yourself repeating this exercise endlessly, even each week, but we have found it worthwhile as it really is an aid to freeing imagination.

✓ *Newspaper Islands* can require a degree of speed and balance. This may encourage quieter and more timid students to be more vocal, excitable and assertive.

✓ *Numbers into a Circle* requires a high degree of concentration and listening skills. As with *Liar*, this exercise benefits from repetition. Some groups will really want to get to twenty and it's a triumphant moment when they do!

Session 5: Listening

INTRODUCTION

It is very obvious on stage when actors are not listening to each other. The focus of the scene is lost, cues can be missed, eyes start to wander and the performance becomes dull and mechanical.

Listening is tied very closely to concentration which people with learning disabilities often find hard.

Sound is something which is easy to take for granted and some of the exercises in this session isolate sounds and ask the students to use them creatively.

WARM-UP

Physical warm-up

It could be useful here to recap or develop the imaginary ball exercise, *Name that ball*, of Session 1 – the ball is heavy, sticky, hot, as light as a feather etc. Make sure the students really listen to the descriptions and keep changing them quite quickly. Focus also on stretching up and down, to 'catch and receive'.

The children's game 'Simon Says' can be a good way of combining physical warm-up exercises with listening skills. A movement should only be done after Simon has given the order, for example, 'Simon says stretch down to the right, Simon says – stretch to the left'. If the call is 'Stretch to the right' no one should move because Simon hasn't given the command.

Vocal warm-up

Using *The Eye of the Circle* exercise from Session 3, students create sounds which are passed on across the circle.

Students in a circle. The first student, call them Number One, begins by choosing someone else in the circle with whom to make eye contact and walks towards them making a sound. Number Two echoes the sound and they meet in the middle. When the sound has been established in the centre, Number One goes to the place vacated by Number Two. Number Two is now in the centre and changes the sound. They make eye contact with Number Three, who echoes the new sound and comes to the middle to meet Number Two, and so on.

EXERCISES/GAMES

1. Sounds in the Room

Ask students to lie down on the floor, in a comfortable position, preferably 'neutral', i.e. flat on back, arms by sides, legs straight out in front. Students in wheelchairs should be asked to find a comfortable sitting position. Switch off the lights or pull curtains to darken the room if possible. Make sure everyone is happy with this before you do so. Some students may have problems with the dark so some light source may have to remain.

Ask students to concentrate on breathing in and out. When focused, ask them to listen to the sounds *inside* the room and to remember them. Now listen to the sounds *outside* the room.

When ready, switch on the lights, ask students to slowly come to a sitting position and individually hear everyone's *listening experiences*. How many sounds were there?

Tools   None, although described as above it can be useful to create a blackout.

Rules   Try to keep eyes closed, body still, concentration.

 Giggling! Remind students to concentrate on breathing in through the nose, out through the mouth.

Variation 'Room Noise' soundtrack. Students have named all the sounds so they now have the opportunity to re-create them vocally.

2. Atmospherics

Discuss the previous exercise. What were all the different sounds that made up the *soundtrack* 'Room Noise'? Shuffling, coughing, noise of footsteps outside, someone calling in the corridor, a car passing in the street, etc. If possible, play the students a tape of different *wild tracks* of films, TV programmes, etc. See what sounds they can pick out and discuss how they might add to the atmosphere of a scene. Then make your own!

Brainstorm possible locations. Jungle, street scene, hospital, battlefield, your own home. Place students in isolation all over the room, or in as large a circle as possible. Ask students to throw their own sounds into the middle, creating the given location's *atmosphere*.

Tools	A tape recorder for playing the demonstration soundtrack and playing back the one you create. A blackout can help to create the mood of certain locations.
Rules	Students must listen to each other to place their sounds in relation to other people's. It may be necessary to brainstorm sound possibilities within each location, and even pre-allocate them, for example, a street scene contains different sorts of cars, one ambulance, two chattering passers-by, a newspaper seller, some birds, a dog and a cat, etc.

 Again, if trying a blackout, be aware of your students' needs. Perhaps use only a dim light, or have a nervous student stay beside you all through the exercise.

3. Soundtrack Story

Students sitting in a tight, listening circle. Begin telling a story. Students have to listen for possible sound effect moments to create, for example, 'The Haunted House' could begin 'One windy (noise) night I was trudging (noise) home, when a car stopped (noise) and the driver asked me the way to the Bates Motel (dialogue).'

Tools	None, although percussion or any interesting sound-making devices could be useful.
Rules	You can either go round the circle waiting for individual sound effects or anyone can be free to contribute at any time.
Variations	(a) Ask students to suggest a title for a story and continue as above.

(b) Once the story is established you can *cast* the sound effect makers and create and record the sound story, possibly *conducting* the sound effect *entrances*.

(c) See if students can repeat the sounds in order from the above *cast* version of the story without listening to the text. If this is possible the soundtrack can be recorded and used in a dramatic reconstruction of the story by the students.

 TEA BREAK

4. Chinese Whispers

Students in a tight circle or line. Number One thinks of a phrase, turns to Number Two and whispers it to him/her. Number Two repeats it to Number Three and so on. How near or far from the original phrase is the message when it gets back to Number One?

Tools   None.

Rules   Students must listen hard to the message and not change it deliberately. Students must whisper or at least speak as quietly as possible.

 Whispering can present a problem for some learning disabled students. Perhaps everyone except the immediate whisperer and listener can block their ears at crucial moments.

5. One Word Story

Students sitting in a circle. Each person contributes one word to the story. One...day...I...was...going...to...the...pub...when...I...met...a... werewolf...and so on.

Tools   None.

Rules   Listen hard, words must follow on and make sense, though they can be unexpected.

Variations Some structure or theme can be pre-arranged.

6. Where Are You, Adam?

Students in a circle. Eve is chosen/volunteers to stand in the centre, *eyes shut* or *blindfolded*. Adam is chosen/volunteers to stand inside the circle. *Eve* calls 'Where are you, Adam?' *Adam* replies 'I'm here, Eve'. Eve is allowed 3 steps to try and reach out and touch Adam following the direction of his voice, before asking again 'Where are you, Adam?' Adam is allowed to move 3 steps before replying. Eve is allowed four attempts at catching Adam before a new Eve is chosen. When Adam is caught, a new Adam is chosen.

Tools   Possible blindfold.

Rules   Strict number of steps.

Variations   (a) Simple version: Adam must stand still.

(b) Hard version: Introduce a Serpent who can call 'I'm here, Eve' from the sidelines if Adam points to him/her.

7. Alpine Calls

Students in pairs. They work together opposite each other echoing each other's sounds or calls. After a while separate them across the room. Those on the left make the sounds, those on the right listen and echo. Change again. Those on the left must close their eyes or turn their backs, and listen for their partner's voice. Swap vocal leaders.

Tools   None.

Rules   Try to listen for the 'space' in which to throw your sound. No two pairings should be making sounds at the same time.

8. Captain's Coming

An old favourite which can be adapted for many occasions and uses listening, concentration skills, mime and bags of energy.

captain – you, usually – stands at one end of room, or high up on a rostrum, giving orders. Students stand facing you in centre of room (as if on the deck of a ship). Orders are explained and demonstrated.

forward – move to front of room.

aft – move to back of room.

starboard – move to left.

port – move to right.

climb the rigging – mime climbing rope ladder.

swab the deck – mime mopping floor.

man over board – lie on floor.

land ho – mime looking through telescope.

More orders can be invented by you and the students.

Tools   None.

Rules   Players must only move if the order is preceded by the words 'Captain's coming!' If a player responds to an order given without the words 'Captain's coming' they are 'out' and must sit at the side. Last person to follow the order is always out until only two players are left.

Variations Title and orders can be adapted, for example, *Christmas is Coming* – with orders such as 'pull a cracker', 'sing a carol', or *Buckingham Palace* with such orders as 'bow to the Queen', 'cut the ribbon' and 'take a photograph', etc.

Skills checklist

✓ Have students listened to the story/to your instructions/to each other?

✓ Have students produced appropriate sounds during *Soundtrack story* and *Atmospherics?* Encourage larger than life sounds. For example, if making the sound of the wind, make it a force ten gale; if making the sound of animals in the jungle, make them stampede!

✓ Have students been able to remain quiet and concentrate on other people's sounds? If students find this difficult, remind them to concentrate on the action of their breathing to focus them.

Skills checklist continued

✓ In *Captain's coming* have they remembered the commands? Start with a maximum of five commands and include the actions in the next session's physical warm-up, repeating the game during the session.

✓ In *Where are You, Adam* and *Atmospherics* how have individuals coped with blackouts and blindfolds? Some students find the idea of not being able to see very frightening. Do not pressurise individuals who show genuine fear – encourage these students to possibly begin by covering their eyes with their hands which may lead eventually to feeling confident with a blindfold.

Session 6: Trust

INTRODUCTION

You will now have had five sessions in which people have got to know each other. In this session they will translate this familiarity into physical trust. Of course, some people are more ready than others to allow physical contact. This session will hopefully help break down those barriers.

On stage an actor needs to know that the whole company is there for you and that everyone is working towards the same end product. In a crisis, it's good to know that others will be able to help cover mistakes, or find a way out of difficulties.

WARM-UP

Physical warm-up

Students in a circle. Each student chooses a different part of the body to warm-up. In turn, each student demonstrates their exercise and the group repeats the action four times. Try to encourage students to isolate all the different parts of the body. A good twist to this exercise is to ask alternate students to try out big then small actions, for example, one stretches up to the ceiling, the next shrugs their shoulders.

Vocal warm-up

Students in a circle. Remind students of the vowel sounds from Session 4. Today we will work on consonants in front of vowels. For example, demonstrate putting T in front of the vowels to make (using fingers to count off as before) Ta, Te, Ti, To, Tu. Ask a student to suggest a consonant and make the sound. Repeat round circle and individually.

EXERCISES/GAMES

1. Back to Back and up and Down

Students in pairs. Ask them to sit on the floor back to back, with knees up and feet planted firmly on the ground. By pressing hard into each other's backs, concentrating particularly on the lower back, and pushing up from their feet, they should be able to come to a standing position. Once this is mastered it should be possible to rise up and down smoothly several times continuously.

Tools	None.
Rules	Encourage them not to use hands to push up from the floor. No giggling, but some communication in the pair helps to establish if the pressure is in the right place.
Variation	Back Lift. Ask about five students to go down on hands and knees side by side, creating a 'table' for someone to lie down on backwards. The 'table' can then gently undulate or rock providing a relaxing sensation.

2. Blindfold Walk

Students in pairs. One is blindfolded, the other is the leader. The pairs carefully make a journey around the room, the leader making sure to lead around any obstacles or other couples in the room.

Tools	Blindfolds or scarves. Possibly taped or live music.
Rules	Ideally there should be silence, but some students may need reassurance from their leader.

 Some students may find it enough just to stand or sit with their blindfold on. In some cases this is a big enough leap of faith.

Variations (a) Create a sensory journey. Using different materials, objects and textures create a pathway around the room that each leader can encourage his/her partner to touch or experience. Anything from water in a bucket to corrugated iron could be used to touch or walk on. It's probably best to do this with each pair going one at a time, with everyone else watching.

(b) In the original walk, blindfold half the group before allocating a partner. See if they can guess who is leading.

3. Trust Circle

Students in a circle. It's probably best not to use everyone in the trust circle if you have a large group. Choose about six of the strongest and most concentrated, ask them to stand shoulder to shoulder with their hands ready to receive and support the person in the centre. Everyone else should sit and await their turn in the centre.

The person in the centre must stand straight with feet flat on the floor, hands by sides, probably eyes closed. Ask them to relax and tell them that friends are there ready to support them and they will not fall. Ask them to begin by swaying very gently from side to side and from heel to toe. The hands of the group should gently add pressure so that the swaying grows in confidence. If very confident suggest they try 'falling' and letting their body relax into the hands of the group, who are ready to push them upright again. Ultimately the body should be given over entirely to the group.

Tools   None.

Rules   This is obviously a very serious exercise and should be done in total silence and abandoned if any giggling starts. You must have confidence in your circle's ability to concentrate and catch. For some people though it is a major achievement just to stand in the group with eyes shut. For others the smallest relaxation of body tension is a breakthrough.

                                                          TEA BREAK

4. Dancing in the Dark

Students in pairs, both blindfolded. Start within reach of each other, or holding hands either sitting or standing. Play music. See what dances emerge in the pairs with different types of music. Gently change the pairings. To finish, gently fade the music and ask the students to come to a stop quietly, preferably sitting down with their partner, before removing the blindfold.

Tools   Blindfolds, different types of music, for example choose music which promotes different moods, dreamy, excited, angry, sleepy, etc. Be inspired!

Rules   Couples must stay silent – no talking or discussion.

 Make sure the working space is clear of chairs and obstacles used in Exercise 2. Be alert – make sure couples don't bump into each other or anything in the room.

5. Tangle and Untangle

Students form a line, holding hands. The leader takes them on a journey round the room, slowly at first, travelling in curves and imaginative patterns. When confidence has been built up they can lead the line under arches of arms, in and out of the line so that people have to twist and turn to follow.

Tools   None.

Rules   No one must let go hands.

Skills checklist

✓ Students should have learned to relax more physically with each other and accept appropriate body contact.

✓ *Back to Back* explored centres of gravity and balance. Have some students been more able than others to trust their weight to someone else? The more nervous or unsteady in balance may need physical guidance to achieve the first 'up' impetus from you in the first instance. However, in the main, encourage support from each other rather than you.

Skills checklist continued

✓ *Blindfold Walk* – if students are reluctant to try the blindfold, don't force the issue. It's one of those occasions when seeing others attempt a task might encourage someone to try something new. When that happens, there's a great sense of achievement all round. *Variation (b)* may make unlikely pairings work for the first time.

✓ In *Trust Circle* has the group been able to take responsibility for an individual? You must continue to stress the importance of their task. It may be valuable to repeat this exercise over successive sessions. There will be some students who find it hard to unbend physically and relax at all but this may become easier with time.

✓ What has *Dancing in the Dark* revealed about students' physical response to music? Also their ability to work creatively in dance with a partner? The darkness often liberates self-expression by eliminating the constraint of self-consciousness and self-image. It may be valuable to immediately repeat the exercise with eyes open and see how responses change.

Session 7: Memory

INTRODUCTION

At this stage it is useful to re-emphasise names and get students to suggest warm-up exercises from ones that they have been given in the past. If a final performance is to be realised, students will have to remember quite complicated series of actions, and possibly lines and cues. This is one of the reasons it can be important to incorporate an element of repetition into the sessions. Students will become comfortable with a recognisable structure and will feel a sense of achievement remembering past warm-up exercises. Memory games are another tool to aid concentration and memory skills.

Talk about the different methods we use to remember things. Tying a knot in a handkerchief, making a list, writing things on our hands, asking other people to remind us. What about numbers and dates? Do we just repeat them over and over in our heads or aloud? Sometimes we remember the pattern of how a series of numbers looks or sounds. Sometimes we associate them with something else. In the *Bathtime for Barbara* game we remembered names through actions.

WARM-UP

Physical warm-up

Give pairs of students a part of the body to warm-up and after brief consultation and experimentation ask each couple to demonstrate and everyone else to copy.

Vocal warm-up

Who can remember a song? See if there is one song that everyone knows. Try singing it in a variety of different ways: loud, soft, as a TV jingle, as an opera. A simple song such as Old MacDonald is an excellent memory game.

EXERCISES/GAMES

1. Kim's Game

A traditional party game that works well in this context.

Students in a circle. A tray is produced holding a number of objects, covered initially with a cloth. Remove the cloth and ask the students to examine the objects and remember them. They may do this by naming them aloud, handling them, discussing them with you. After several minutes the tray is recovered and students are asked to name the objects.

Tools Tray and objects, for example, a clock, a flower, some stamps, an eggcup – the more outlandish the better.

Variations (a) This can be played as an individual or team competition.

    (b) The objects can all be related and can be the basis of a story or improvisation.

    (c) One or more objects can be removed and the game is to work out which ones are missing.

2. My Grandmother went to Market

Students in a circle. You begin with the phrase 'My grandmother went to market and bought a...' And add a purchase, for example, a cabbage. The next student must think of a second object and add it to yours: 'My grandmother went to market and bought a cabbage, and a magazine.' Continue round the circle making the shopping list grow longer until it reaches you again, whereupon the whole team can repeat the entire list.

Tools None.

Rules It may be appropriate to have a time limit for thinking of a purchase before moving on to the next person, or it may be better to ask the hesitant student to mime an object, or to take suggestions from the other students and ask him/her to choose one.

Variations The purchases must be named alphabetically, for example, 'an apple, three bananas, some curtains...' or the title can be

changed, 'I went on holiday and packed...' 'I went into
hospital and I met...', 'I journeyed into outer space and I
saw...' or ask students for their suggestions.

3. Clothes Basket or the Magic Box

Another exercise known by a variety of names, excellent for memory work
and for introducing the concept of mime.

Students in a circle. Take a mimed object out of the basket, use it, put it
back, pass the basket on to the next person. When the basket comes round
full circle the process begins again, and this time each person must take out
something which *someone else* has put in.

Tools   This game works best using a physical container in which to
find mimed objects. Anything from a clothes basket, to a
plastic bag to a handbag can be used.

Rules   The ritual is part of the game; the taking out and the putting
back each time should be observed.

Make sure your bag is *empty*, otherwise unexpected discoveries
can prove distracting!

TEA BREAK

4. Grandmother's Story

Remembering the list of objects that were in Grandmother's shopping list
(or whatever) before the tea break, divide the class into two and ask each
half to come up with a little improvisation, each using all of the objects in
turn.

Tools   None, although props could be used if available and
appropriate.

Rules   Every item mentioned must be used, the more outlandish the
context the better!

Variation   A verbal story could be told instead.

5. Appealing for Witnesses

Students sit opposite the door, or 'stage' curtains if there are any. Select one student to go out, before you tell the other students the object of the game – the element of surprise is all! When the student has gone out, tell the others that they are police witnesses and they must describe everything they can about the person who has gone out: clothes, height, hair colour, and so on. Student returns and see how accurate the group description has been.

Tools   Possibly a chair. The returning student may feel more comfortable sitting down when he/she is re-scrutinised.

Rules   The student must remain behind the door until called back in by the group. A carer may possibly have to accompany .

Variations (a) As the game goes on, and people get the idea, the group description can become individual descriptions.

(b) In pairs, sit/stand opposite each other and study each other carefully. Then, in turn, put each student back to back, *with the rest of the group watching* and let the group question them about each other, for example, 'Lionel, what colour shoes is Tom wearing?' 'Tom, is Lionel wearing his glasses?'

6. Detective

Students in a circle, you are in the middle and act as The Detective. The students must act as one person with a joint memory – they must remember what facts have been established and not contradict them.

Make up a short statement of why you are questioning them. For example, 'There was a serious murder in the park last night and we believe that you could help us with our enquiries'.

Possible questions:

- What is your name?
- How old are you?
- What is your job?
- What is your home address?
- What were you wearing last night?
- Where were you last night?

- What were you doing there?
- Were you with anyone?

Tools   None.

Rules   Everyone must listen to what is being said as you can repeat questions to try to catch people out.

Variations If anyone contradicts themselves more than three times then that exposes them as the murderer and everyone shouts 'SEND THEM DOWN' and a new game begins.

7. Farmer, Pig, Wolf

A good game with which to finish the session, as it involves movement and noise after quite a concentrated and static couple of hours.

This exercise is a kind of physical variation of the game Paper, Scissors, Stone.

Ask students to make a frozen picture mime of a *farmer* – could be someone digging. Next, a frozen picture of a *pig* – usually hands up to ears for little pig ears. Last, frozen picture is of a *wolf* – usually hands out like paws, snarling face.

Practise saying as a group 'Piggy, piggy, piggy, one, two, three'. Once students have mastered this, split up into two equal teams facing each other at either end of the room. Ask teams to walk towards each other until they meet in the centre of the room whilst saying 'Piggy, piggy, piggy, one, two, three'.

Once this has been achieved, ask them to repeat the above but this time when they meet in the middle they must take up a frozen position. First try everyone being a *farmer*, then a *pig* and next a *wolf*.

The overall idea of the game is to try to get students from the other team onto your side. To do this each team must brainstorm in a huddle or scrum to decide which frozen picture they are going to be from the above. They then walk towards each other saying the practised rhyme at the end of which they, as a team, take up their individual pictures.

Farmers can catch pigs before they run back to base.

Pigs can catch wolves before they run back to base.

Wolves can catch farmers before they run back to base.

Tools   None.

Rules   Farmer takes the pig, the pig takes the wolf but the wolf takes the farmer. Everyone in each team must be miming the same picture.

Skills checklist

✓ Has concentration been maintained in studying the *Kim's Game* objects and remembering the items in *Grandmother's* list? The team option often helps with this. Also the more attractive and incongruous the items the better the chance of capturing interest and retaining the image.

✓ In *The Magic Box* have students been able to think of an object to take out? If not, ask group members for suggestions. It is a good idea not to reveal the second part of the game (i.e. taking something out that has already been put in) until the first round has ended. This adds an element of surprise and makes students think harder. If students can't picture any of the original objects, ask, 'What did so-and-so put in?'

✓ Have students been able to focus on each other's work? Some students with learning disabilities need to be the centre of attention, so exercises such as *Appealing for Witnesses* can be quite challenging for those jointly putting the picture together – the 'attention seeker' clamouring to contribute everything. It's probably best to give them the first turn out of the room so they see how they game works while being the first person 'in the spotlight'. Meanwhile, the rest of the group will have had a chance to give the descriptions one at a time.

Session 8: Feelings

INTRODUCTION

The expression and sharing of emotion is one of the key things that makes an actor interesting to watch. It is not easy for anyone to open their feelings to outside scrutiny, even if they are hiding behind a character. Therefore it is OK to acknowledge this to yourself and your students and not expect to be able to share feelings instantly.

People with learning disabilities often have particular difficulty in this area. Ironically this can be because emotions in life – for example, anger, affection – are often more on the surface, and they have become accustomed to being asked to modify their feelings to a socially acceptable level. Perhaps a lot of the work in this area will be concerned with assuring them that this is a good and safe place to explore feelings, and to channel them into a creative expression.

WARM-UP

Physical warm-up

On this occasion it is probably best to start the session with the first exercise, as the second, *Hugging and Stroking*, is something that can take up an unquantifiable length of time and should be explored at its own pace.

Vocal warm-up

A vocal exercise after *Hugging and Stroking* could simply be to vocalise, with one sound or word, a response 'How are you feeling today?' and to look at where in the body the resulting sighs grunts and groans stem from.

EXERCISES/GAMES

1. Response Sculpture 1

Such sculptures can be used at any time to ascertain how the group is feeling about a particular issue. Today we will just ask the question 'how are you feeling today?'

Tools	It can be quite useful to use an object, for example, a chair, as the fixed point from which the sculpture is measured.
Rules	Students nearest the object are feeling positive about their day. Furthest away, are not so happy. If appropriate, time should be taken to discuss these feelings, find out the causes. Even if you feel powerless to help concretely with any specific issue, it is important to give the students an opportunity to vocalise their emotions. Make them feel it's safe to talk. Obviously if something very serious emerges you must discuss it more fully with the individual, possibly at tea break, or another date, and possibly make contact with the student's keyworker.

2. Hugging and Stroking

Students in pairs. (A and B). Ask them to go to the edge of the room, next to a wall or something that can comfortably support the back. A sits down with back to the wall, B sits down and is cradled and supported by A in a comfortable almost foetal position, head on chest or lap. A soothes and gently strokes B.

Tools	None.
Rules	Absolute silence. After some time ask students to swap roles. Trust your instinct and allow enough time for this exercise to take its course. We have often allowed time upwards of half an hour. Eventually invite the students to make a circle and ask them about the experience – suggest they give one word responses. Words that emerge can be 'supported', 'safe', 'like a baby'.

3. Response Sculpture 2

Repeat of first exercise. It will be interesting to see if, or how, feelings have changed after Hugging and Stroking.

TEA BREAK

4. The Oh Game

Students sitting in a circle on the floor. Introduce three balls and give each of them a different emotion, for example, sad, happy, frightened. As each ball is passed round, students must say 'Oh' as they individually pass it on, registering the emotion.

Tools   Three balls or different objects.

Rules   The balls can either be passed round one at a time (probably the best way to start), or they can be passed simultaneously.

Variations The game can be played with music, as in *Pass the Parcel,* so that when the music stops everyone can really listen to the sounds.

5. Emotional Statues

This game uses the same format as the party game Musical Statues. When the music stops, or you call 'Stop', name an emotion which the students must represent physically, particularly using their faces, for example, happy, sad, angry, etc.

Tools   Tape recorder with music.

Rules   .   The statues should be still and silent.

Variations Make a mental note of individual statues. Ask for spot demonstrations at the end of the game. Make sure the statue is the same as its original – memory test.

6. Emotional Photographs

Recap with students different emotions that have already been discovered during the previous exercises. Students in threes; director and two models. Name an emotion. The director must place the models into a 'photograph' illustrating the emotion. It can be abstract or tell a story.

Tools   None.

Rules   It is often valuable to have a look at an interesting 'photograph' and ask the others to comment on it. Ask them what the 'title' is and see if it corresponds with the 'director's' idea.

 Some students find it very hard both to choose their models and then to give them instruction. Stress that part of the challenge is for them to exercise their authority (politely!) and to develop their own idea. Try to get close friends to choose another member of the group.

Skills checklist

✓ Some of these exercises can be very revealing. Have there been any unexpected emotional reactions to *Hugging and stroking?* How have you dealt with it? Usually individuals feel warm and secure after this exercise but occasionally some deep or hidden trauma can surface. Make sure you deal with such a situation appropriately. You may need to stop the session, call a tea break and talk in depth about the problem on a one-to-one basis. From there you can decide what further action should be taken and whether another agency should be informed. Other students can also have a profound reaction to someone else's upset – so it's wise to be prepared for any eventuality and feel confident about your own responses. This is another reason why this exercise should only be attempted if there is sufficient time.

Skills checklist continued

✓ How did students react to taking direction from a fellow student in the *Emotional Photographs?* If they are finding it difficult, stress that it will be their turn to direct or lead the action soon.

✓ Have faces been used in *The Oh Game* to register emotion? Try suggesting the ball has some animate life, for example, 'it's a sad cat' or 'It's a poisonous snake'. Similarly in the *Emotional Statue,* you may need to personalise the emotions, for example, 'You're Happy!' 'You've won the Lottery!' For some reason, the learning disabled students we have worked with are all eager National Lottery players!

Session 9: Sounds and Rhythm

INTRODUCTION

Music, sound and rhythm are often an important aspect of any performance. Taped or live music can create mood within a scene and in between scenes (and of course can be a useful cover for scene changes). It can also be inspirational for dance pieces. Self-expression using voice and instruments, especially percussion, can be very liberating within a workshop situation and in performance. The music performance group Heart and Soul[1] (a professional company based at the Albany in Deptford employing musicians/singers/performers with learning disabilities) are an excellent example of this.

Rhythm exercises can bring a group together, and the creation of a sound/rhythm piece gives everyone a sense of achievement and can be an exciting part of any performance. Therapeutically, emotion can be released through the use of instruments and new 'voices' can be found.

If you have a particular skill in this area yourself, you will be able to explore further, or collaboration with a music specialist can prove very exciting.

WARM-UP

Physical warm-up

Exercises for opening the chest, feeling flexible and ready for anything.

Students in a circle. Skiing exercise: standing tall, arms up, swing down, bend your knees, arms back, head down, and stand up. Repeat. When your arms are above your head for the second time, swing them down and round in a circle, in front of your body twice (like a windmill), ending up with arms above your head for a third time, and if possible stretch the body up onto tiptoe.

[1]   Tel: 0208 694 1632

Feet together, standing straight, arms stretched out, hands together in front of you. Breathe in, take one arm straight back over close to your head and point it out behind you, breathing out to a count of three. Let your arms flop to your sides. Repeat with the other arm.

Feet apart, one arm hangs down close to your body, the other above your head stretching over to the other side. Bounce gently. Repeat on the other side. Practise the above taking deep breaths in and out, and with the hand that is hanging down feel the lower ribs, which should be opening and closing.

Vocal warm-up

Work in pairs. Place hands on partner's ribs – feel how each others' ribs move in and out. Make sure shoulders remain still and necks free with no straining and tension.

Students in a circle holding hands with eyes shut. Ask students to remember the *Oh Game* from the previous session. Ask students to open mouths wide and let an OH sound come out. 'What did that sound like?' 'Was it a first thing in the morning OH, or a last thing at night OH or something else completely?' Decide as a group what it sounded like. Next, suggest, as before, different emotions and ask the group to make collective sound but this time elongating the sounds. The group may feel like carrying the sound into their arms, swinging them in the air with each new sound, whilst still holding hands and making a group movement.

Now take a neutral OH. Ask students to drop hands and open eyes. Ask them to breathe in through their noses and out through their mouths to your count. The in breath can be the same each time – we suggest a count of 'breathe in two, three, hold two, three and OH two, three, four, etc.' Increase your count out – see if the group can get up to as high as twenty! Repeat with the other vowels as in the A E I O U exercise from Session 4.

EXERCISES/GAMES

1. Spiral Sounds

With one hand point to the ground. Begin an 'Aah' sound looking and pointing at the ground (it will probably be a low note). Spin your finger like a top from the ground, progressing to above your head and hear how the note changes (usually higher). Take the sound and movement behind your head, 'catch' it before it vanishes, and 'throw' it forwards. Catch it again. Repeat, starting with different vowels or sounds, such as 'shhhhh'.

Tools	None.
Rules	The movement displaces the focus from the sound, making a free, or less self-conscious sound. Remind students to open their mouths as wide as possible and let out 'warm' sounds (Remember the two-finger drop).
Variations	Take sounds in different directions: behind you, sideways, to the floor – listen for the different sounds.

2. Sound Symphony

Students in two or more groups. Choose a conductor or take the role yourself. Give each group a simple rhythm, or let them choose their own, for example, easy clapping, slapping knees, patting hollow cheeks. The conductor starts the first group off with a 'downbeat' of the hand. They continue clapping unless indicated to stop with a 'flat' movement of the hand (side to side). The second group is told to begin and so on.

Tools	The conductor could use a baton or stick.
Rules	All instruments in the orchestra must keep strictly together. With confidence smaller sections of the orchestra can be created.

3. Name Rhythm

Students in a circle. Each person thinks of a simple action rhythm that corresponds to the number of syllables in their name; for example, Barbara Darnley could be three claps followed by two stamps. Go round the circle discovering names and rhythm actions and repeating them in groups of four.

Tools	None.
Rules	As in *Bathtime for Barbara* when you reach the last person in the circle go right round again remembering everyone's names and actions in one go.

Variations Try to repeat the sequence of actions *without* the names to guide you.

TEA BREAK

4. Cookie Jar

Students in a circle. Give everyone a number. Start a slow, regular rhythm, for example, two slaps on the knees, two claps. Now teach the chant, which must be strictly in time to the rhythm you've set up.

> Who stole the cookie from the cookie jar?
>
> Number 2, stole the cookie from the cookie jar.
>
> Who Me?
>
> Yes You.
>
> Not Me.
>
> Then who?
>
> Number 9 stole the cookie from the cookie jar.

Tools None.

Rules There must be no hesitation. If someone hesitates before choosing a number to 'accuse', they are out. If they say their own number or the number of someone already out, or if they get the format or words wrong they're also 'out'. Needless to say this takes some practice, and quite a lot of trial runs are needed to crack the game.

Variation Once people are really good at this you can add the following complication. If someone makes a mistake they must go to the end of the line and take over the last number; for example, in a group of 10, if Number 4 makes a mistake they must go to the end position and become Number 10. Thus everyone else's number also changes, and concentration skills are really tested.

5. Eurovision Song Contest

Split up into groups of approximately three. Each team is a pop group from a different country. The bands must individually brainstorm, choosing a country of origin (could be imaginary), a name for their band and a tune that they all know. Each group must develop a language to sing in, and rehearse the presentation of their song (maybe with dancing). After a given time each group presents their entry to the others. A voting system takes place with individual votes cast for the band that has just played. Points could be awarded out of 10 for Concentration, Presentation and Star Quality.

Tools　　Props could be used for 'microphones', etc.

Rules　　Care must be taken to stick to the 'language'. The groups will need your help with this in rehearsal.

Skills checklist

✓ Did *Spiral sounds* free up people's voices? Perhaps begin the exercise by asking for several large first-thing-in-the-morning yawns. 'Begin by stretching and making a vocal yawn as if you were still in bed.'

✓ In *Sound symphony* were sections of the 'orchestra' able to stick together and keep in time? You may have to start with a very slow, simple rhythm, possibly with the whole group to begin with and split the group up gradually. It could help to isolate the smaller groupings initially so they don't get distracted by other rhythms until very secure in their own. You could also divide the group into two and sit back to back to learn their own patterns.

Skills checklist continued

✓ *Name Rhythm* usually works with enough repetition (it's also a good name reinforcement game). If the group has particularly disparate physical mobility you may have to ask the more mobile individuals to offer a pattern that everyone can follow with reasonable ease, or again ask them to demonstrate their sequence very slowly to begin with.

✓ *Cookie Jar* demands quite a high level of concentration, verbal and rhythmic skills – lots of professional actors find it very difficult! However, it's a good warm-up on these three levels and also as a group bonding game. It may not be suitable for everyone – you will be the best judge here, but remember, some learning disabled students can completely take you by surprise so in general we recommend you have high expectations.

Session 10: Basic Improvisation

INTRODUCTION

In recent years improvisation has taken on a life of its own as an entertainment in its own right at comedy venues and on television. Techniques evolving from everything from *Commedia dell' Arte* to the Marx Brothers make us gasp at the performers' ability to think on their feet and create situations from nowhere. Most of these seemingly effortless talents start with the basic premise of working with your fellow actors and accepting what is offered and building on it.

This can be quite a hard concept to get across to some people with learning disabilities. Some people can be extremely creative and imaginative on their own terms but find it hard to accept someone else's fantasy. We had a student whose every improvisation involved a horse, another whose every situation ended in deliverance by James Bond (it is quite common for students to resort to television references), a third who inevitably took the scene into a hospital. On the other hand some people find it impossible not to relate every scene to their own environment and experience.

If you are working towards a performance the chances are it will grow from the students' own work and creative contribution, rather than a script you provide. You may well formulate a draft to refer to, but probably this will be based on the students' individual talents and may not be appropriate for another group. So getting to grips with the basics of improvisation will yield dividends in the long run.

WARM-UP

Physical warm-up

Musical instrument warm-up. Following on from Session 9's musical theme, in a circle, each person takes it in turn to use their whole body in an enlarged or exaggerated way to play a different musical instrument; for example, if they chose a piano, this could involve running sideways to cover all the keys with their hands. Or if a trombone, think about breath and go forwards and backwards. Each movement is led by a group member around the circle and is repeated eight times.

Vocal warm-up

Students form a circle. Take it in turn to call out a word. The group has to repeat/echo the word as one large group. Then repeat the above but this time the group echo calls out the word's opposite. It might be necessary to brainstorm as a group after a word has been called out so that everyone is saying the correct opposite – for example Hello/goodbye, hot/cold you will find some words have to be re-chosen as they might not have an opposite, for example, fire engine.

EXERCISES/GAMES

1. Presents

Quite simply, you mime giving someone something; for example, a bunch of flowers. The receiver must say 'Thank you, what lovely flowers. They smell nice.' Or 'Thank you, they are my favourite colour, yellow', and so forth.

Hold hands out. Size of gap between the hands gives some idea of shape of present. Receiver has to invent present. Try to make reaction as enthusiastic as possible. To begin with it is often easier if you demonstrate. For example, 'Oh thank you Ali, what a lovely kitten.' Mime stroking kitten. 'I've always wanted a pet of my own, how clever of you. It's so small and soft, and listen everyone she's purring. I'm going to call her Ripley.'

Tools	None.
Rules	We've found the exercise works best with students in a circle, crossing one at a time to give someone a gift.
Variation	If students are having difficulty with imagining what the present could be, try brainstorming and write down a list of presents people would like to receive and simply pick them out.

2. 'I'm Sorry I Broke Your...'

This game follows on well from *Presents*. It appears relatively simple, but incorporates good improvisation technique. Everyone we have worked with has readily related to it and found it accessible and amusing. Humour is often a stimulating way of freeing up self-consciousness and allowing focused participation.

A has to invent something B has lent him. Introduce the idea by saying that the object lent to A by B, was either extremely valuable or of sentimental worth to B.

The conversation could go something like this:

'You know that camera you lent me last week?'

'Yes, the one my mother gave me before she died'.

'Well, I'm awfully sorry, I've broken it.'

B has to decide whether to be sad/furious/generous in their loss.

'I don't believe it (tears)/how could you, it was of huge sentimental value/that's OK, it was only a camera.'

A continues the conversation.

'I'm so sorry, please don't cry/I don't know what to say, I can't believe I was so stupid/I'll buy you a new one, etc.'

Rules   A must have an attitude to the loss – working on emotions. *B* must invent object and a tale about its loss/destruction.

Tools   None – the object is imaginary and mimed.

 It has been our experience that in some instances students may find it difficult to come out of the improvisation: this can apply to several of the exercises in this session, so it may be necessary to help the student to de-role. A useful way of doing this is to employ a relaxation exercise. Whilst standing, ask everyone to shut their eyes – or for those who have difficulty with that, to concentrate on one thing/object in the room. Talk them through listening to their breathing and to the sounds that are inside and outside the room. Ask them to stretch gently, to yawn, and to circle their arms, waving out the feelings and to begin to be themselves again. It is important to take as long over this as you feel is necessary.

3. Ironing Board and Horses!

Students in a circle. A comes into the centre and takes up a definite physical position, for example, bending over. B comes into the middle and relates to A in some way. For example, A's position might suggest an ironing board, so B will begin ironing, or a horse, so B could pick up a hoof and shoe it. When B has 'used' A, A can leave the centre, B strikes a pose and then C comes in, and so on.

Tools   None.

Rules   This can be done verbally or non-verbally.

Variations C could come in and instead take A's place and become another object, for example, a wheelbarrow, which B would then have to use. Perhaps then you could send D in, who would take B's position and maybe drive a car and so on.

4. Commercial Break

Brainstorm ideas for adverts. You could bring in magazine pictures, or show a video compilation of some TV adverts for inspiration. Divide the students into groups and ask them to come up with a new product to promote. If this is too hard they could choose one they already know. Suggest different ways of presenting the product – jingles, cartoon style characters, authoritative boffin recommendations, spoof film genres, etc. When each group shows its work you could vote on the desirability of the product in the 'Eurovision' way, giving categories such as mouth-wateringness, most catchy tune, glamour, etc. to decide if the advert has been successful.

Tools   Any props could be useful.

Rules   Set up, or ask the students to imagine their presentation acting space is the size of a TV screen. Tell them to present the advert clearly to the audience so that anybody sitting at home in front of their screen could see every movement and hear every word, without turning up the volume! This will make them aware of the basics of projecting volume and not blocking each other's actions.

TEA BREAK

Many of the exercises in previous sessions have emphasised the importance of listening and co-operating with your fellow actors. The next two exercises are verbal games which practise the habit of accepting suggestions from someone else and building on them.

5. Accept and Build

Begin with telling a chosen student that they must agree with everything you say!

> You: 'Hello, I met you at the party, you're John aren't you?'
>
> John: 'Yes.'
>
> You: 'You work in the supermarket.'
>
> John: 'That's right.'
>
> You: 'It's your birthday today isn't it?'
>
> John: 'Yes.'
>
> You: 'How does it feel to be twenty one?'
>
> John: 'Great thank you.'
>
> Once they've got the hang of that, the next stage is to repeat the above and add something about you or them.
>
> You: 'Hello, I met you at the party, you're John aren't you?'
>
> John: 'Yes, you're Barbara, right?'
>
> You: 'Yes, don't you work in the supermarket?'
>
> John: 'That's right, I help pack bags, you work in the bank next door'.
>
> You: 'Yes, it's your birthday today isn't it?'
>
> John: 'Yes, I'm having a party tonight, do you want to come?'
>
> You: 'Yes please, how does it feel to be twenty-one?'
>
> John: 'Great thank you. See you tonight!'

Tools   None.

Rules   Students must accept what is said. If students are having problems with this, change the rule so that each person must begin what they say with 'Yes and...'. Time is well spent on this concept as it is the basis of successful improvisation. Actors must accept what is 'Offered'[1] and either go with the premise or build on it so the scene becomes something else. Some people with learning disabilities will find it hard to accept even the simplest unreality such as accepting a different name, but it is worth persevering.

6. Send a Letter

Students sitting in a circle. One student volunteers to be 'postman'. The 'postman' collects a letter from the 'sorting office' (you), walks around the outside of the circle and chooses an 'address' to stop at. The 'postman' knocks on the door by stamping their foot behind the chosen person who then stands up and collects the delivery. This person reads the letter aloud to the group – possibly with your help. The letter could be along the lines of:

Dear Pat,

I cannot come and visit you today as I am very tired. Yesterday when I went to the bank to pay in my wages something terrible happened as I was waiting in the queue. Two people came in and started shouting. They told us to get on the floor and not move. Then they told the cashier and the manager to get the money from the safe. They were robbers. I shouted for them to stop but they told me to shut up. Then the police arrived and arrested them. The manager had been able to touch the alarm button.

See you next week.

Love Jo

The letter reader casts the characters in the story from the students in the circle. They act out the story in the centre. When they have finished, another postman 'collects' and 'delivers' another letter, and so on.

1   See Keith Johnstone.

Tools   A selection of letters written by you. Props may be used from things around the room or from objects that you have brought.

Rules   It is important that the action stays inside the circle. Those watching must concentrate on the action.

Variations With some students you may find that it is not necessary to provide written letters. The exercise works well with students using an imaginary letter and making up their own original stories.

Skills checklist

✓ In *Presents* have students managed to invent an object? Some may not be able to immediately – ask them about their last birthday or Christmas; what did they get? Take them back through that moment of giving and receiving.

✓ Those for whom the choice of gift is easy should be encouraged to create a more elaborate scenario in *'I'm Sorry I Broke Your…'*. Their challenge is to explore confrontation, emotional reaction and spontaneity. Often students will just say 'That's OK. I don't mind if it's broken' or 'Sorry'. Talk them through how they might feel about a personal gift or possession which they treasure.

✓ Were students able to associate actions/situations with the physical shapes made in *Ironing Board and Horses?* You may need to ask the group for collective ideas and suggestions for transformation, or ask a student who has an idea to 'sculpt' someone else into a position. For some students it will be a development even to put their body into an unusual shape. As in *What are you doing?* or *Liar!* in Session 4, some students will find it hard to change from one action to another. Persevere, maybe even repeating it next session, and this exercise will pay dividends.

Skills checklist continued

✓ In *Commercial Break* did students succeed in selling their products? Canvass opinion between the groups: 'Would you buy this?' In any event, they should have enjoyed the challenge.

✓ *Accept and Build* is the basis of all improvisation. Were students able to accept a given which was not their reality? Again, some students will find this concept difficult. It is sometimes a good idea to give examples of conversations which enormously differ from reality until they get the hang of it. Sometimes the most unreal of suggestions are more readily accepted than those which are closer to the truth. For example, 'Your name is Cool Banana and I met you yesterday on the moon didn't I?' rather than 'Your name is Suzi and I met you in the supermarket yesterday, didn't I?'

✓ In *Send a Letter* were students able to develop a narrative of their own, however simple? You could take them through a letter they might receive, such as an invitation to a party or a hospital appointment.

PART II

Progressing and Developing the Work

Exploring Theatre Skills

ROMEO
AND
JULIET'S
WEDDING

Session 11: Introducing or Finding a Theme

At the beginning of this book we stated that the end result of the workshop structure would be some kind of performance. However, it may be that a public showing of work is not possible within the confines of your organisation, or again, not appropriate to your group. Don't shut the book now. It is more than likely that working towards an end product is enough of a goal in itself, or that many of the exercises and techniques that follow can be adapted to an ongoing drama workshop.

For this section of the book, the content and format of each session will vary with the choice of theme. You will know the best place to break for tea at a midway point during your workshop.

Begin the session with a lively game such as Fruit Salad, and/or the following physical warm-up.

PHYSICAL WARM-UP

Students in a circle. Assuming there has been a break since the last session, ask people to re-create a movement relating to their holiday, for example, driving, flying, putting on sun tan cream, surfing, skiing, being at a funfair. First student reduces their chosen movement to an essential action which everyone then copies, repeating the movement eight times. Go round the circle until each student has led the group.

Split the class up into pairs who stand opposite each other. Using only *four* of the movements identified, each pair must develop a movement 'dance' sequence, mirroring each other. Either let the leader organically change, or call out 'Change' to give each partner a turn at leading.

Then ask the students to add a vocal to their physical movements – any sound they feel like; emphasise there is no right or wrong.

EXERCISES

1. Fruit Salad

(If there are wheelchair users or people with mobility difficulties this game is possible but not ideal – you could use another lively game such as *Captain's Coming* from Session 5 instead).

Students sit on chairs in a circle. You are in the middle without a chair. The object of the game is *not* to be left in the middle without a chair!

Ask the students to choose four fruits, for example oranges, apples, bananas, pineapples. Go round the circle giving each student a fruit in turn, and take one yourself.

Double check that everyone knows what fruit they are, by saying, 'Apples, put your hand up; hands up if you're a banana', etc.

When you call out a fruit or combination of fruits, those fruits must leave their seats and find another empty one. You, as the person in the centre must always try to find a seat. The person left without a seat in the middle then calls out the fruit combinations, for example, 'Apples!' 'Bananas and oranges!'

When the call is 'Fruit salad' everyone changes seat.

2. Ideas Session

form a circle for a discussion. At the end of the last session you discussed with the group a possible structure for the next two terms and asked them to think, over the break, about possible themes or stories to work on. Emphasise that they can be in control of the next two sessions and that this is a great opportunity for everyone to contribute to the creative process and help choose the subject of the forthcoming project. Your group may not respond to this – it could be that you will eventually have to impose your structure and ideas, but on the other hand you could be very surprised at the definite ideas people have, and your own preconceptions about themes may have to take a back seat.

3. Brainstorming

Possible tools: pen and paper notes/flip chart and marker for general referral; tape recorder to make verbal notes/record.

Has anyone come prepared with an idea? Acknowledge and record it. Discuss/decide in advance, as appropriate, the following topics:

- Is there going to be a public/invited audience?
- What are the expectations of the group: do they wish just to explore and enjoy further acting skills or are they burning to address a particular topic or story?
- If it's an issue-based piece are the issues general or specifically related to learning disabled people?

Bring in pictures from books or magazines to promote discussion. Let's imagine that brainstorming came up with the following ideas: Holidays; *Neighbours; Eastenders;* getting a job; bullying.

You suggested themes from *Romeo and Juliet,* or maybe a narrative poem such as *The Ancient Mariner* to dramatise.

Discuss the pro's and con's and preferences for different themes.

4. Soap Opera

This seems to be a frequent suggestion. You'll need to discuss why people have suggested a soap opera – it's popular entertainment which many people enjoy watching. However, the form is more suited to ongoing improvisation rather than an end performance. You could use the structure of a soap to dramatise issues which interest the group. But you'll need to emphasise that it could be more fun to choose your own characters rather than ready-made ones from TV. It can be great fun and stimulating to create a whole new world of characters in their own environment, choosing a name for the town, pub, shop, etc. and all the recognisable locales of 'soapdom'. The improvisations can then go on for a period of weeks, each time with a new theme.

It can be interesting to record on tape or video an episode at the end of each session and listen/watch at the beginning of the next. We have particularly found that this works extremely well when working with people with very limited physical mobility. The majority of group members enjoy listening to the episodes.

5. Tackling the Themes

As one large group, brainstorm some physical ideas for each theme. Choose four themes/ideas to present as quickfire improvisations. Split students up into four groups and see what they come up with. You can go round and give them help, but divide groups so that there is someone quite able in each as a 'leader'.

Here are some ideas for tackling basic scenes which give a quick sketch of each theme.

HOLIDAYS

Find out about individual different experiences – choose an element of one to physicalise, for example, checking in at airport, a boat trip, a coach journey, a beach episode, ordering food in foreign language, etc.

Cast a scene, for example, *at the beach*. Someone swimming, sunbathing, ice cream sellers, etc. Pinpoint an incident on the beach – could be naturalistic, for example, a chat-up on the beach or outlandish, for example, a tidal wave that sweeps everyone away.

GETTING A JOB

Again, discuss personal experience – job interview, training, dressing the part, first day at work, down the pub with work colleagues, etc.

Cast a scene, for example, the *interview*. Set up a desk and chair. Perhaps brainstorm together some of the questions that might be asked. Include the ritual of knocking on the door and being invited to sit down. Try the scene with a pre-decided job, and again leaving the nature of the job up to the players to decide.

ROMEO AND JULIET

If the group don't know the story, do a quick essential précis: two people meeting at a party and falling in love; families not approving; telling of arranged marriage, etc.

Perhaps improvise the *wedding*. Cast the bride, groom and priest (Friar). Discuss the fact that it's a secret ceremony; how will this make the trio feel? Will there be anyone else there? Perhaps other students could sing or make sounds of a distant choir.

Discuss Juliet's relationship with her parents and the idea of arranged marriages. Improvise a confrontation around this issue, or any relevant parent/teenager cause for stress.

ıg party; meeting strange old man; ıts; game of dice; killing of the

ling with a happy crew and the d feeds. As a movement exercise, oving vessel.

for next week which theme they :o remember what they did today ı further in the next session.

Pages 86/87 – themes
— What would you do differently?
section.

Page 89 – Emotions (didn't give them a character teacher said they'd struggle) ⮕ do that differently next time.

Pg 96 – Tribal chant & tribal challenge.

Page 107 – Box of tricks (similar to compound stimulus).

Page 109 – difficult adopting a character. ⮕ Why change? Talk about film characters.

Session 12: Building Confidence and Presentation

PHYSICAL WARM-UP

Students in a circle.

Who remembers what character they played last time? Using these characters and choosing exaggerated movements they might make, students take it in turns to go into the centre, demonstrating an action each, and the rest of the group copy the movement, for example, sailor climbing rigging, priest bowing, holiday-maker swimming, and so forth.

VOCAL WARM-UP

Re-create the sounds of the storm, perhaps with everyone sitting on the floor close together in a circle with eyes closed.

Re-create the sounds of an office/shop/other work environment, perhaps with everyone in a line choosing different sounds, such as: knocks on the door; phone ringing; typewriter; fax machine; coffee maker; till; tannoy.

Re-create the sounds of a church: echoing with prayers, chants, footsteps, murmurs, organ. Create the chanting of nuns/monks or a wedding hymn.

Re-create the sounds of the beach: waves lapping; seagulls; children laughing; dogs barking; foghorn; coach party arriving.

EXERCISES

1. Presentation of Self to Group as Audience

Again, using the themes and characters from the previous session, work on different ways of presenting self, starting from the simplest walk across the room or entrance into the room.

Example characters:

- Bride and Groom
- Sailors
- Interviewer
- Interviewee
- Holiday-makers.

Look at how these characters move. Repeat the exercise but this time give the characters different emotions, such as:

- Scared
- Confident
- Relaxed
- Aggressive
- In love
- Shy.

2. Scenes

Recap scenes from last time. Have another look at them. Perhaps recast them, giving everybody an opportunity to try out different parts. Perhaps swap scenes between the groups, seeing what interpretation another group gives to a different scene.

Ask the whole group to comment on the work in progress. Could they understand exactly what was going on each time? The *Who, Where* and *Why? Who* was playing what? *Where* were they? *What* were they doing and why?

If some of these issues were unclear – explore.

Could everyone be heard? If not, was it because some people were not talking loudly enough? How clear was diction? Did anyone have their back to the audience inappropriately? Was eye contact maintained when people were speaking to each other? Did people give each other space to talk? Were relationships properly introduced and maintained so that you knew who each character was? Was the location obvious? Were any pieces of furniture placed correctly, so that characters could relate to each other and be seen by the audience? Was the story of the scene clearly told so that you could see not only what was happening but also understand why?

In other words, talk the group through elements of *directing* the scenes, letting them discover why some things worked wonderfully, as well as how some things could be improved.

Look at the scenes again in the light of the exploration you've just been through. For the last 10 minutes or so of the session, discuss the work so far and see whether any clear preferences or suitability of theme have emerged.

3. Storyboarding

A whole session could be spent on this. Alternatively, you could incorporate the method in helping to script, or describe, either certain sections of the piece, or the whole thing.

Many people find visualisation of the story or script an extremely useful device for keeping the whole concept in their heads. It's a technique used widely in the film and television world.

Break the story or scene down into key moments of action. Take a large piece of card or several pieces of A4 and draw simple pictures delineating the story. Each picture need be only very basic, using stick people as characters. The effect is similar to a cartoon strip.

Alternatively, give each of the four groups the materials to create a storyboard for each of the four themes. Thick felt pens and large pieces of paper are most practical. Suggest they come up with a maximum of six pictures per theme. Even if individuals are not able to draw, or do not want to contribute artistically, most will be able to help with ideas for each picture. When enough time has been spent, you can discuss each group's visual ideas with the whole group, asking for comments, interpretations and further ideas on each set of drawings.

4. The Way Ahead

By the end of Session 12, you will probably have come to a firm, or nearly firm decision about the theme of your project. Your group's own timetable and goals will dictate the urgency of the decision.

For the purposes of this book we are going to describe the process of working through two very different projects, 'Holidays' and '*Romeo and Juliet*'. We will describe exercises and rehearsal techniques for both themes, which will of course also be applicable to other projects. We have chosen 'Holidays' because it is a fairly all-encompassing title, that will appeal to, and have personal resonance for almost any group, and could also lead to issue-based work. '*Romeo and Juliet*' is a given text that has already been interpreted in so many different ways, its application is universal.

In Sessions 13–20 we will be working on different theatre skills. We will describe skills to be explored, and often apply them directly to both the themes.

Session 13: Progressing from Movement to Dance

We all rise to a challenge. Do not make the mistake of thinking learning disabled people are any less capable of aiming high. In our experience they can do more, not less, than some other people with influence in their lives generally expect. Movement and dance can be extraordinarily liberating – do not be afraid to take some risks. Really encourage physical exploration and push students to their limits.

WARM-UP
Waking Up

Ask everyone to begin by lying on the ground. If there are any wheelchair users ask if they feel able to join you on the floor (this may be only advisable if mats are available, and if getting back into the chair is reasonably easy). Many wheelchair users welcome the opportunity to do floor work.

Demonstrate stretching, curling, twisting – almost as if you are doing a series of 'good morning' stretches in bed, but at three times that speed. Use arms and legs to explore the space on the floor to the left, right, above and behind you. Sounds will probably be released as well.

EXERCISES
1. Only Connect

Get everyone up from the floor. Ask them to move swiftly around the room, thinking privately about one particular *person* in the group. On your command (drum beat, clap, vocal command to 'Hug' or 'Meet'), students should go as quickly as possible to the person they've been thinking of and give them a quick hug. On another command, they should move off again and start thinking of someone else. It doesn't matter if more than two people join together. After a while change the instruction. This time ask people to think of a *place* or a spot in the room. On the next command, they should go immediately to it. Next, join the two things together. A third command, means thinking of someone and taking them to your pre-decided spot. This results in struggling, stretching, lifting and running, as well as the necessity for someone to acquiesce in each partnership.

2. Name Dance

Students in a circle, or four groups. Remind them of the dance they created using their own names in *Name rhythm* (Session 9). This time introduce prepared music. Make a tape of music reflecting different moods or emotions – sad, happy, excited, frightened, etc. See how the dance changes with different music. If working in groups, give everyone an opportunity to watch each dance.

3. Holidays

Movement work based on a holiday theme could take you in all sorts of directions. Here are a few ideas. You will soon decide which sort of 'holiday' the group might be taking.

SUMMER BEACH HOLIDAY

Think about the sights and sounds of the sea. Line up four of the group lying on the floor and encourage them to roll over and over, stretched out, rolling backwards and forwards in the rhythm of waves. Something similar could be devised with a group standing or sitting – a kind of Mexican wave. Different tempos, representing different moods of the sea could be explored.

A WINTER HOLIDAY

A collage of winter sports movements could be devised – tobogganing, skiing, skating, throwing snowballs, snow boarding. Or the whole group could be a giant toboggan.

A group of tourists could create a 'photo-opportunity' dance. Perhaps they are taking pictures of famous monuments – bodies could be used (remember making an electrical appliance in Session 1) to create a Tower, a Pyramid, a Bridge, etc. Or the camera clickers could concentrate on simply taking photos at the same time, while bending their bodies into different poses.

4. Romeo and Juliet

Decide on a scene to illustrate – we have chosen the Ball and the fight; you could also explore the wedding and the funeral.

THE BALL

What sort of a dance/party is it? Start by playing some current dance favourites and let the group dance in their own style. Play the soundtracks of different versions of Romeo and Juliet, for example, Prokofiev's ballet, Bernstein's *West Side Story*, Baz Lurhman's film soundtrack, and see what different styles and moods they evoke.

Then play different sorts of dance music through the ages. Perhaps Elizabethan, a 'Jane Austen style' formal dance, a waltz, an English or Scottish country dance, a Charleston. Demonstrate basic steps. Decide on whether the dance you are creating is to be a couples dance or a circle dance.

A country dance may be easiest, using pairs who also join hands in a circle. Great fun can be had, particularly if you are careful with the pairings and have at least one in each who can follow and remember basic steps.

THE FIGHT

Explore different types of fighting – no doubt there will be lots of suggestions incorporating guns. Encourage other ideas – swords, hand to hand, etc. and break each one down into essential elements – perhaps using slow motion. Each person could create their most grisly, physically stretching 'death'. Perhaps divide into two teams – Montagues and Capulets – and create a fighting movement sequence using partners.

Demonstrate some of the basics of stage fighting:

a)   the blow to the stomach that stops short

b)   the slap across the face that misses and has a sound effect created either by the victim hitting their upstage leg at the same time as receiving a slap on the face, or by the victim facing upstage and clapping as they are 'hit'

(c)   the kick to the stomach when the victim is on the ground, where the kick stops short of contact

d)   the stage fall – collapsing from the knees and sinking down onto the fleshy part of the hip first

e)   the stage fall – being caught by someone else. This person stands behind ready to support the weight as the victim falls backwards.

Introduce some music and explore how it affects the different movement sequences you've come up with. Alternatively, play different passages of music and see what 'fighting styles' are suggested by it.

Session 14: Discovering Your Voice

WARM-UP

The vocal exercises in this session are all concerned with centering the voice and helping to increase confidence and volume.

EXERCISES

1. Tribal Chant

All in a circle. Set up a rhythmical movement/stamp/shuffle to the right. Add in some kind of vigorous arm movement, possibly suggesting harvesting, mowing, sweeping. Begin a full-throated call that must be repeated by everyone in rhythm (a similar feel to the 'give me an 'A' – 'Aayey' feel of political demonstration chanting). Immediately the chant has been repeated, the person on your right should begin with a new sound. The movement helps to deflect any mental self-consciousness about the voice.

2. Tribal Challenge

Split the group into two. Each group becomes a 'gang' who creates its own chant – could be like a war cry or maybe a football chant or slogan. They also invent their own way of moving in unison – perhaps shoulder to shoulder or arms linked, so they can function as one unit. Each group then moves around the room communicating, possibly challenging the other group, but only by using the pre-discovered chant. You could set a rhythm for movement using a beat or drum.

3. Wishing Well

Students in a circle, possibly sitting on chairs. Ask them to imagine the space in front of them as a large, echoing well. One after another, ask them to send a wish in the form of a sound down into the well, first as a whisper, and then, as it is a very deep well, louder and louder, so that the wish reaches the bottom of the well. When the wish is as loud as it can possibly be at that moment for that individual, send the sound echoing back 'up' to them. It may be appropriate for you to help earlier than this by encouraging the sound into the well, so that the individual is joining your voice sending sound forward and downwards.

4. Basic Alexander Technique and Relaxation

If students are comfortable working on the floor ask them to lay down flat on their backs. Now place a medium-size book, or another sort of rest, underneath the head, not the neck, so that the head is in line with the rest of the spine, not stretched back as it would be without support. Next ask them to raise their knees, with feet parallel, and then drop their feet flat on the floor, knees pointing to the ceiling. Arms should be lying loosely by sides, with a gap under the armpit big enough to accommodate an imaginary orange or grapefruit. Hands should perhaps be lightly placed on belly/centre to achieve this. Eyes should be open to encourage focus on the body rather than sleep!

From this position talk them through each part of the body, starting from the toes and on through up to the head, asking them to imagine each area spreading out and releasing onto the floor, the spine lengthening.

While in this position begin vocal exercises, such as gentle focus on breathing, followed by vocalised exhalations, first on an SSS then a ZZZ and then an Aah.

When you ask them to rise, make sure they get up slowly, preferably by rolling first onto the side, then coming to all fours and standing slowly so that the head is the last thing to come up.

5. Find Your Centre/Address the Audience

Ask the students to find a space at one end of the room, or if you are working in an auditorium, facing the audience. They should stand in the neutral position, ready for anything! Ask them to think about the parts of the body that will help to create a great sound – beginning with the knees!

- They should have *Squeezy Knees*, slightly bent, not locked, so that the body is relaxed, weight forward on the toes rather than heels.

- They should have *Feet under Bottom,* body straight but not ramrod.

- They should have *Sunny Tummy*. This is where the centre of emotion, focus and therefore sound starts. Ask them to rub their belly, imagining it as a smiling powerhouse of energy.

- They should have *Alive Eyes* showing that they're ready to communicate.

- They should have *Relaxed Shoulders*, the breath coming from the diaphragm and ribs not the throat and top chest.

Now ask them to pick a spot or a seat in front of them and address that spot with all the excitement and desire to communicate possible. There's a story that needs to be told. Choose a simple phrase, 'Hello My name is…', is as good as any, or a line from a known text such as 'All the world's a stage', or a line from something they are working on.

After a while get everyone to sit down in the audience position and ask individuals to take centre stage and deliver their phrase – a bow and a round of applause will encourage even greater enjoyment in new-found power.

6. Open Vowels

A good and gentle way of creating a relaxed sound with an open throat is a 'smiley sigh'. In the neutral position breathe in through the nose, and with a slight smile sigh out gently on a 'Haah' sound. This raises the soft palette, creates an open 'tube' to the diaphragm through which breath can flow, and produces a calm, warm sound, very good for pre-show nerves. You will find your eyes smiling too and a general feeling of alertness is induced. You could describe the gentleness of the sound you are after as a 'Tellytubby' sound!

7. Breath Control

Another 'Haah' exercise, but now with a stronger sound – good for breath control.

In the neutral position breathe in through the nose and breathe out to increasing counts, i.e. your instruction would be: 'Breathe in 2, 3, hold 2, 3, and out on a "Hah" 2, 3. Breathe in 2, 3, and hold 2, 3, and out 2, 3, 4. Breathe in 2, 3, and hold 2, 3, and out 2, 3, 4, 5', and so on. Vowel sounds should be made with open mouths (a two-finger drop – make the shape of a gun with two fingers for the barrel and put it upside down between front teeth).

The use of the letters S and Z is excellent for pure breath control stamina.

8. Nasality

An excellent way of demonstrating nasality in a voice and showing how to produce a forward sound rather than a nasal one is to explore the phrase:

Away by the shores of far Brazil

Say it:

(a)   normally (but with attention to the richness of the vowels)

b)   holding your nose and sending the sound out through the nose

c)   holding your nose but directing the sound out through your mouth.

It is perfectly possible for (a) and (c) to sound the same.

Perhaps finish off the session by singing something everyone knows. Most people know 'London's Burning' and if the group is feeling adventurous you could turn it into a round.

Other rounds are 'Rose, Rose', 'Frere Jacques'. A scale song is 'Old Abraham Brown' and fun action songs are 'The Frog Song' and 'The Elephant Song'.

The exercises above are very much a selection from which to pick and adapt to the needs of a particular group. Any two of them could potentially take up a whole session.

Session 15: Status and Mime

Discussion and exploration of status within a scene can often help the actor establish who is in control of the situation, how the scene is driven and also the psychological relationship between the characters. Learning disabled people are often not as aware of these issues in daily life as other people. Generally they find it easy to relate in an uninhibited way to anyone they meet, and complications of class and status do not clutter their personal relationships. On the other hand, they may not be used to taking control of situations and for this reason status exercises can be a liberating experience.

Status can often be complicated and sophisticated, but on a basic level it is simply about who is in control or in charge, at any given point in time. It can be interesting and fun to experiment changing this. How do you know who is in control? The most instant way of recognising status is to look at somebody's physical demeanour.

An example of this can be seen in a country such as Japan, where people bow to each other when greeting and saying goodbye. The deeper, longer more frequent bow indicates that that individual realises they are lower in status (standing, importance) than the other.

The classic exercise with which to explore status is the master/servant relationship.

EXERCISES

1. Master/Servant

Split the group up into pairs. A and B. A is the Master, B is the Servant. Ask A to think of 10 things that they want B to do. Swap over. If people have problems with this they can imagine that they are the King or Queen with a footman/servant – we have found most students easily relate to this.

2. High and Low

A physical status game. In pairs, think of couples whose physicality demonstrates high and low status.

- The Queen shaking hands with a member of the public on a walkabout.
- A pop star giving an autograph to a waiting fan.
- A politician giving a press briefing.
- A judge sentencing a prisoner.

How does someone's physical demeanour demonstrate their status?

3. Door to Door Selling

A verbal battle of wits! Using status to make someone buy something they don't want.

Two players – a buyer and a seller. The encounter could take place in an open doorway, or just as a conversation. One student is selling something – for fun, make it something outlandish such as blue chickens! The seller thinks of clever ways to make the buyer buy the goods – perhaps saying the chickens are fresher than those from the supermarket. 'Everyone who is anyone is buying these chickens – the feathers make wonderful pillows.' The potential buyer has to make a good case for not buying the goods offered without simply 'closing the door'. They must think of reasons to reject the 'once in a lifetime offer' – thus getting the better of the other and achieving higher status.

4. Swapping Status Mid-Way

One large group. Brainstorm pairs of characters – one with high status, the other with low. Students can choose examples from the *high* and *low* list and add their own. Write them down on a piece of paper and put them in a 'hat' and let pairs of students pick one out. Brainstorm locations and then write them on paper and put into the 'hat' for selection. Pairs rehearse their high/low status improvisation within the given location.

These short scenes are presented to the group. Look at them again, and at a given moment call *freeze*, and tell them to swap status whilst remaining in the same character. Students may need extra help and guidance with this exercise because of the number of tasks they should be focusing on at the same time. However, in our experience, we have found this exercise particularly useful. For example, students such as Wilson and Tim B who have problems accepting authority had the chance both to exercise it and be on the receiving end of it, whilst remaining the same character.

5. Job Interviews

In pairs explore:

- A very high-handed interviewer who intimidates the job candidate. How would you react? By being cowed or standing up for yourself?
- A rude/shy interviewee – what kind of impression does each make? How does the interviewer cope? Playing high, low or equal status?

Rehearse the above and then present to group. All these status exercises provide invaluable improvisation experience and are also a good opportunity to demonstrate how to direct – through stopping and starting, and changing and developing the scene.

6. Romeo and Juliet Status

Brainstorm with students examples of status within *Romeo and Juliet*. In groups or pairs improvise the following situations:

- Parents and children. Invent a battle of wills between parents and teenagers – about staying out late/unsuitable boy/girl friends/clothes. How to deal with different views and reach a compromise.
- Masters and servants – the Capulets and Montagues are rich and may have servants. How do they treat them?
- The Prince of Verona and his subjects – how does he show his status and how does he use it? Is he a good or a bad ruler?
- Gangs. Tybalt as the leader of the gang with his followers.

7. Holiday Status

Again, brainstorm with students' examples of status within the Holiday theme. In groups or pairs improvise the following:

- At a holiday destination invent two types of 'eaterie'.

- A very upmarket restaurant with different waiters to pull back your chair, take your order, pour your drinks. Are the diners comfortable with this or do they feel intimidated? High status or low status?

- A very relaxed beach café, where the food is slapped down, the service sloppy, the meal unsatisfactory. Do the diners meekly accept everything or do they complain? High status or low status?

Session 16: Style

Theatre and all forms of drama involve representation, and style is the way in which it is displayed or shown. Remind students of the work done earlier in presenting themselves neutrally to an audience – how important the way they moved and talked was. Very simply, different styles involve different ways of moving and talking.

By theatrical style we mean the historical differences in the subject matter of plays and in acting methods and tastes. Thus a 'Restoration style', coming from an age where plays were the provenance of the court and wealth, has an easily recognisable flamboyance and obsession with manners. Melodrama, catering for a Victorian taste for the lurid, often has recognisable stock 'hero and villain' characters. Some of the plays of the 1950s are called 'kitchen-sink' drama to indicate not only the apparent ordinariness of their themes, but also the naturalism of the acting style required in playing them.

It's unlikely that many of your students will be regular theatregoers. However, most of them will have a good knowledge of TV and films, and their love of them may be one reason why some of them have come to your workshops. They will recognise quite easily the style and genres of different films and this is a good place from which to begin a little exploration of theatrical styles.

EXERCISES

1. Film Night

Begin the session by discussing students' favourite films. Compile a list and look at what makes each film different. Ask the students how they would describe the film, for example, comedy, drama, thriller, film noir, horror, period, action movie, domestic naturalism, etc. You may find that all the students like the same sort of film – it could be the most recent blockbuster/action movie. You will need to encourage students to choose different films covering a variety of styles and may need to suggest others that they might have seen. For comedy, most students will have seen a 'Carry On...', for horror, an old 'Dracula...', etc. on television.

Three students, the 'directors', select two or three others to work with on their chosen film. They work together on presenting a very short one-minute favourite 'clip' which is representative of the style of the movie.

You could take the role of a Barry Norman type character and put together a film 'programme', with you introducing the clips and the students presenting their favourite movie excerpts.

If you have access to video equipment (see Session 20), it can be extremely good fun and a valuable learning tool to film this session.

2. Video Night

This exercise can only work if you have access to at least a VHS video player and monitor or television – if you are working in a Further Education College or Day Centre, do not forget to book your equipment well in advance.

Bring in films that you have chosen which clearly illustrate different styles, and show some extracts. For example we have found *Mission Impossible* (thriller), *Naked Gun* (comedy), *Braveheart* (period) Kenneth Branagh's *Much Ado About Nothing* (Shakespearean style) and his Mary Shelley's *Frankenstein* (horror), also any film by Mike Leigh (naturalism), particularly useful.

The Channel 4 comedy improvisation programme, *Whose Line is it Anyway?* was being shown when we last worked on style. There is a game in which the four contestants improvise a scene which the host keeps interrupting. Each time he interrupts, the actors must change the style of their performance from a list taken from audience suggestions, for example, comedy, horror, Star Trek, etc. We taped this part of the programme to show to the students, and because of the larger than life performances it was a very graphic demonstration of different theatrical styles.

As an instant practical demonstration, you yourself could perform a monologue, poem or even rhyme, for example, Happy Birthday, in different ways.

3. Whose Line is it Anyway?

You could make up your own game of it with the students as above, with you calling out the different style genres which you have made up, or use students' previous suggestions.

4. Tea Time

Split the students into pairs. Each pair is given a cup and saucer as a prop. Most Further Education Colleges and Day Centres have a canteen, so simply borrow as many cups and saucers as you need, making sure you promise to bring them back at the end of the session or at tea break and do actually take them back!

Below are some suggestions; you will be able to think of more.

- Naturalism – the couple use the props in an everyday scene, for example, over breakfast, maybe they are happy, maybe they are having an argument. In the latter how could the prop be used? As a weapon?

- Comedy – the prop helps create something which is funny, maybe two people who meet in a café on a blind date. There is mistaken identity involved and confusion over whose tea is whose.

- Slapstick – invent different routines with the prop itself being the object of fun. Maybe it starts talking? Maybe it keeps flying off in different directions (make sure students keep hold of it!).

- Thriller – maybe the cup has a bomb inside it – *Mission Impossible* style.

- Horror – the cup is full of poison.

- Romance – the cup becomes a symbol of a couple's love.

- Period – the tea drinking is a social art, for example, in the plays of Oscar Wilde.

You could use the techniques of Forum Theatre here (see Bibliography: any books by or about Augusto Boal). Stop and start the scenes, put new people into each role. Change the director.

5. Sword-Fighting (see Romeo and Juliet)

Bring in lots of old newspapers – broadsheets work best because of size. Tightly roll the papers into long tube shapes and secure the join with sellotape. You will find that they are quite strong and become like virtual swords.

Split the students into pairs and stand each couple opposite each other in two lines. Demonstrate the basic actions of lunging, parrying, thrusting and being on guard. Practise advancing and retreating.

You may well need to cover this if you choose to do a project such as *Romeo and Juliet*. Or perhaps your performance will have a surreal element or dream sequence in which there is sword-fighting. Most learning disabled students don't often get the opportunity to be physically confrontational with each other. This exercise allows them to explore some physical conflict in a safe environment.

6. Adverts Anonymous

Using adverts as a starting point, try to re-create them using different styles. We have had great fun working from students' suggestions. A classic example is the old Milk Tray advert – with the man in the black polo-neck jumper – which most people remember. Play it straight as action/romance/thriller, then play it again as zany comedy where everything goes wrong and the girl is sick when she eats the chocolates. Another more recent advert that springs to mind is the romantic Gold Blend series. An interesting twist could be to play it as period drama.

7. Working Towards Performance

Ask students to select, or choose yourself, some scenes already devised from your performance project and change the style of them. Often this can be a useful learning experience for all concerned. You may make new discoveries, especially about a scene with which you have been struggling.

8. Box of Tricks

Fill a large box with different costumes and accessories that suggest different characters and styles of work. A good selection from the following could be useful: practice skirts (long full-cut skirts), wigs, fans, tunics, cloaks, swords, hats, guns, masks, handbags, cigars, cigarettes, sunglasses, glasses, different shoes and boots with varying heels, etc.

With the box in the centre and students in a surrounding circle, take it in turns to try something on. See how it affects the way that the student feels and moves. (This can also be a good exercise to use in Session 17: Building a Character.) Put various characters together in a situation and ask if the costumes and props suggest any particular style to the students. Set up a series of short, quick-fire improvisations with the emphasis on style.

9. Four Scenes

Split the students into four groups and give each a situation and style which they have to present in an improvisation. These four situations could be:

- Railway station. There is an international spy present. The spy is trying to get on the train without a ticket. Some undercover agents from MI5 are following the spy. Present this in the form of *thriller*.

- Castle on hill. The king is in despair because no one wants to marry his daughter. A list of potential suitors is drawn up and they are presented to the princess for her to make a choice. Present this in the form of *pantomime*.

- Classroom in college. The teacher is taking a maths class and two students are being disruptive. The head of department is sent for and a warning is given. Present this in the form of *naturalism*.

- Big top. There is a group of acrobats who are too old to tumble but try to do what they can with great panache. Present this in the form of *circus*.

Session 17: Building a Character

Acting always involves taking on a role. Even the film stars who play 'themselves' are in fact selecting which of their own characteristics to present to the camera. It is easier for some people to adopt a new character or persona than others. We have found that some learning disabled people find adopting a different persona or character a challenging task. Some students find even the simple concept of taking on a new name frightening, perhaps it seems to challenge their own identity, but this session will give you ideas and exercises to confront these issues.

In our experience a useful way of opening this session is to talk with the group about their favourite TV or film characters. Why do they like who they like? Who are those people in reality? Do some of these actors play more than one character? For example, George Clooney as Batman and as Dr Ross in *ER*. Barbara Windsor in the Carry on films and as Peggy Mitchell in *Eastenders*.

The discussion around Building a Character will probably include the following:

- Age, background, voice and accent, where have you come from prior to each scene, where are you going after each scene?
- External characteristics: walk, mannerisms, facial expressions, posture, health, etc.
- Internal characteristics: intention, intelligence, sexuality, feelings and emotion, attitude, etc.
- Costume: clothes, shoes, hats, etc.
- Props and accessories: umbrellas, walking sticks, pipes, cigarettes, glasses, handbags, fans, etc.

- Overviews: choosing one word to describe each scene or section of performance.

EXERCISES

1. Shortcut Characters

Shortcuts for identifying characters can be useful to explore. Ali, a student obsessed with James Bond, simply has to turn up his collar and mime a cigarette in one hand and a gun in the other to become 007.

Shortcut characters: Popeye, Charlie Chaplin, Eric Morecambe, Superman/girl, Long John Silver, Dracula, Frankenstein, the Queen, etc.

2. Funny Walks

Students moving around the room in different directions imagining that they are in a park. Begin with neutral walking, then call out different instructions:

Walk as if...

- you are very old
- you have sore feet
- your shoes are too small
- you have high heels
- you have a limp
- you are pigeon-toed
- you are a Sergeant Major
- you are the Queen
- you are a ballet dancer
- you are a cowboy
- you are a tramp
- you are a spy

We have found that a good variation or extension of this exercise is for the group to sit in a semicircle facing the door and ask for one student at a time to go out and come back through the door as one of the above. Students must guess who they are by how they are walking.

3. Mannerisms on a Bus

Students in a circle. Ask them to look around the circle at each other to see if they can identify any personal mannerisms that you or others students may have. If nobody has any, invent some. Brainstorm a list of mannerisms to work on. These could be big or small and include some of the following:

- a pronounced sniff
- clearing the throat
- tugging at your clothes
- scratching your nose
- scratching any part of the body
- an eye that twitches
- leaving your mouth open
- sticking out your tongue
- blowing your nose
- sucking your teeth
- holding your head at an angle
- shrugging your shoulders
- grinding your teeth
- spitting
- making unusual noises
- burping
- particular ways of using your hands/gestures.

Students choose from one of the above, or from their own suggestions and sit on the bus. A conductor is chosen and has to guess which mannerism the student has chosen whilst asking for the fare.

4. Voices and Accents in a Pub

Ask students about their favourite pub or club. Discuss characters they know who have different sounding voices or accents. See if they can demonstrate. Set up a pub improvisation with these characters. If the students cannot think of many, suggest television characters, for example,

Cockneys in The Queen Vic in *Eastenders* and Mancunians from The Rovers Return in *Coronation Street*, and so on.

TEA BREAK

5. Cinema Queue

Four students stand in a line and they each have to think of a different character – it can be someone they know. They must become that person, and from their outward appearance the rest of the group has to work out what sort of character they are by assessing their body language, their mannerisms, anything they might say to each other. We have found that it may be necessary for you to give each student a character. Take it in turns in groups of four, so that every student tries this out.

6. Hot Seating

As a group to make a list of twenty general questions to ask a character. For example:

- Where were you born?
- How old are you?
- Where do you live?
- What is your job?
- Are you married?
- Do you have children?
- How long have you lived where you live?
- Where did you go to school?
- Do you have brothers and sisters?
- Are your parents still alive?
- What do they do?
- Describe your house.
- Where did you last go on holiday?

- What is your favourite meal?
- Do you have any pets?
- Describe your favourite outfit of clothes.
- Do you drink a lot?
- Have you ever been involved with the police?
- What is your religion?
- What star sign are you?

Obviously these are just a guideline. At the end of the prepared questions there could be an opportunity for people to ask their own questions.

Another idea, or one to use at a later stage when the parts are actually cast, would be to tailor specific questions to each character, for example, in 'Romeo and Juliet' you could ask Juliet:

- Have you ever had a boyfriend?
- Describe your ideal man?
- Do you get on with your Mum/Dad?
- Who do you spend most of your time with?

Or address the following to Lady Capulet:

- Do you have any children?
- How many servants have you got?
- How long have you been married?
- Describe your wedding day.

7. Coping with the Media

Whenever anything happens to anyone famous, or any public figure, newspapers, magazines, radio and television reporters always want to publish the facts, or 'dish the dirt'. For example, when Princess Diana died, everyone who had ever known her was interviewed for their story and their feelings.

You could create two magazine interviews with, say, Lady Capulet. One, a lifestyle magazine finding out about her home life, furniture, hobbies, make-up, dinner party guests, holiday destinations, fashion sense. All these are superficial qualities, nevertheless they all add up to creating knowledge of a character. The second could be a more harrowing interview with the distressed mother after her daughter's death, such as you might find in a tabloid newspaper.

Questions could include:

- How did your daughter die?
- How did that make you feel?
- Describe your emotions when you saw her body for the first time?
- Has this affected your relationship with your husband?
- Did Juliet have many relationships with young men?

8. Physicality

Here is an exercise demonstrating three different ways of exploring a character's physicality. Think of an everyday situation that involves movement, for example, getting up in the morning.

(a) Select one character from your performance project, for example, Juliet: then everyone explores how Juliet might get up in the morning.

(b) One student plays Juliet and everyone else watches how she gets up in the morning, possibly making suggestions and comments.

(c) Everyone selects a different character and they all explore getting up in the morning at the same time.

Talk the students through a series of actions appropriate to the example, for example, yawning, stretching, getting out of bed, washing, dressing, coming downstairs for breakfast.

Constantly side-coach the students to focus on their character's physical movements by asking questions such as:

- How old are you?
- Would you be moving that fast?
- Are you glad to be getting up?
- What clothes are you putting on?
- If you are stretching, how far can you stretch?

9. Design a Costume

Two different ways: talking it through verbally or providing everyone with paper and pens and time to draw a picture of their character; or alternatively, you could draw on a large flip chart taking instructions from students' ideas.

10. Performance Theme: Brainstorming

In this exercise you could relate background and social standing to characters in your own performance project.

For example, from the *Romeo and Juliet* theme we began with Juliet's father, Lord Capulet. What is he like? As a group we brainstormed what we knew about him.

What are the basic emotions/feelings he expresses at given points in the story? For example, he's an outgoing Lord of the Manor type at beginning; in charge and a bit of a bully making Juliet marry someone she isn't keen on; bossy when he is ordering around his servants; very charming and 'smarmy' to Paris – the man he wants his daughter to marry; angry with Juliet for refusing to marry Paris and furious with Romeo and his friends for gatecrashing his party; very sad when Juliet dies.

Draw comparisons with students' own lives. Has anyone felt like a 'Lord of the Manor'? How did it affect the way you walked and talked? Demonstrate.

Session 18: Using the Right Words

TECHNICAL TERMS USED IN THE THEATRE

The theatre, like every other profession, has its own jargon. Many theatrical terms are common knowledge, a few are obscure. Most are a form of shorthand. If you pass on some of the correct terms to your students you will find the directing process a little easier. If you are working in a professional theatre space you will be able to speak the same language as the permanent staff.

1. Theatre Personnel

- *Director* – chooses the actors, directs the show, has final say in most matters.
- *Producer* – in a big organisation finds the money/backing to put on a show.
- *Stage Manager (SM)* – is in charge of running the show backstage.
- *Deputy Stage Manager (DSM)* – works closely with the actors and director in rehearsal, prompts, passes on information to other staff about new props. During performances runs the show i.e. gives lighting and sound cues from the prompt corner.
- *Assistant Stage Manager (ASM)* – runs around a lot! Finds props, makes coffee, helps actors backstage, in charge of props backstage, often moves scenery on-stage.

2. The Theatre or the House

- '*The house is open*' indicates the audience is allowed to come in and the actors should no longer cross the stage.

- *Curtain-up/down* is the start/end of the show. *'What time does the show come down?'* i.e. What time does it end?

- *Dark* – if a theatre is dark there is no performance that night.

- *The show* – any theatrical performance is known as a show be it a play/dance piece or whatever.

- *Front of House* is the area of the building for the public, i.e. auditorium/foyer/bar.

- *Box-office* is where you buy your tickets.

- *To paper the house* is to give away tickets free in order to secure a good audience.

- *The pass door* leads from the auditorium to the side of the stage, or front of house.

3. Inside the Auditorium

- *The pross.* is the proscenium arch between the audience and the stage. Most old theatres were built like this.

- *In the Round* some performance spaces have the audience on all sides. They usually then take place on a flat surface and the audience is *raked,* i.e. angled away.

- *Traverse staging* has the audience on two sides.

- *The iron* is the safety, fireproof curtain that can divide the audience from the stage. This, by law, must be lowered in front of the audience at every performance.

4. On-stage

- *Entrance* – the door or place from which to come onto the stage/space – *to make an entrance*

- *Exit* – the door or place from which to leave the stage – *to exit*

- *Forestage/thrust* – area of stage which juts out into the audience.

- *The rake* – the angle of the stage in relation to the auditorium.

- *Upstage* – the area away from the audience.

- *Downstage* – the area nearest the audience.

- *Stage right* – the right hand side of the stage when looking at the audience from stage.
- *Stage left* – the left-hand side of the stage when looking at the audience.
- *Prompt corner* – usually stage left, from where the DSM runs the show.
- *Wings* – areas out of view of the audience at each side of the stage.

5. Working on-stage

- *Blocking* – the rehearsed pattern of movement on stage.
- *Business* – plotted piece of action, often extraneous to the plot but that adds interest to the scene – especially used in comedy.
- *Corpsing* – laughing inappropriately on stage individually and with fellow actors as a private joke.
- *Cover* – another word for an understudy.
- *Cues* – the signals to speak, act, or do something technically, for example, a lighting change.
- *To be DLP* – to be dead line perfect.
- *Lines* are the text of the script.
- *To mask someone* – to hide them from the audience.
- *To be Off* – to miss your cue to come on stage.
- *To project your lines* – to speak loudly and clearly without appearing to shout.
- *To prompt* – to give someone his or her line.
- *To strike* – take a piece of scenery or prop off-stage
- *To upstage someone* – to pull focus away from them onto you, often by standing upstage from them.

6. Backstage

- *Backstage code* – to be quiet in the wings; not to block an actor's path to an entrance; generally not getting in the way.

7. Calls

- *Calls* – time schedules. An actor's rehearsal call is the time at which to be at the rehearsal room.

- *Beginners call* – five minutes before the start of the play the actors should be in place backstage. They are given a *five-minute call* ten minutes before the start and a *half-hour call* thirty-five minutes before the start. Actors should always be in the theatre before *the half*.

- *Curtain call* – taking a bow.

8. Rehearsals

- *Marking out the set* – indicating on the floor of the rehearsal room the position of the set, usually with pieces of different colour tape.

- *Run-through* – rehearsal with lines learnt and no stopping.

- *Stagger-through* – stopping run-through with lines imperfectly learnt.

- *Line-run* – rehearsal for lines only.

- *Technical rehearsal/tech-run/the tech* – rehearsal primarily for the technical crew to practise lighting/sound/stage effects/costume changes and for the actors to use the stage set, often for the first time.

- *Dress-rehearsal or the dress* – final rehearsal with costume.

- *The prompt-copy* – the stage-manager's copy of the text with all the cuts, actors' moves, lighting and sound cues marked in it.

- *The Green Room* – is a room backstage in most theatres where the actors and crew can relax.

- *The Dock* – where the scenery is stored.

9. Lighting

- *Lamps or lanterns* – stage lighting.

- *Spots* – spotlights.

- *Follow-spot lime* – a hand-operated spotlight.

- *Gels-filters* used in front of the lantern lens for colouring.
- *Batten* – the barrel or tube from which a piece of lighting or scenery is hung.
- *Clamp* – attaches the lamp to the batten. There should also be a *safety-chain.*
- *The gantry* – the bridge on which some lanterns are hung/placed; also called the *catwalk.*
- *Plotted* – sequence of lighting. The final sequence becomes the *lighting plot.*
- *Practicals* – lights on stage, for example, a standard lamp that can be switched on.
- *Talloscope* – a safe moveable ladder/platform which technicians use to hang or *angle* lamps.
- *LXQ* – a lighting cue is indicated thus in the prompt-copy.
- *FXQ* – a sound cue.
- *Maroon* – a bomb effect.

10. Props

- *Props* – properties or physical objects used by actors on stage.
- *Practicals* – props that need to work, for example, a kettle that has to boil on stage.
- *Dressing* – any physical object on stage that adds to the look of the scene but is not used practically.

11. Scenery

- *Backdrop* – a piece of painted cloth scenery at the back of the stage.
- *Cyc or cyclorama* – a large piece of cloth stretched across the back of the stage instead of a backdrop. Lighting effects can be projected onto it.
- *Flat* – a piece of flat scenery made of painted canvas on a frame. It is held up by a brace or a triangular support often steadied by a heavy *weight.*

- *The Flies* – the large area, often a *fly-tower*, above the stage from which scenery and lighting can be hung and lowered to the stage. *Flymen* do the work, pulling on ropes or *hemps* in older theatres.

- *Gauze* – a transparent or semi-transparent piece of material through which action can be seen indistinctly.

- *The get-in / get out* – when the scenery is taken in/out of the theatre.

- *Masking* – a piece of scenery or curtain that hides the actors from the audience at the side of the stage; usually not an integral part of the stage design.

- *Riser* – a small rostrum or a measurement of a tread.

- *Stage cloth* – a covering for the floor of the stage.

- *Treads* – are steps on stage.

12. Curtains

There are innumerable names for different pieces of cloth! Here are a few.

- *Blacks* – pieces of usually black cloth used as masking. Stage management also wear *blacks* (black clothes) backstage.

- *Boarders* – mask the tops of flats. If not made of cloth they are *headers*.

- *Drapes* – curtains on scenery windows.

- *Drop* – can be a lowered cloth.

- *Legs* – black curtains at the side of the stage for masking, usually flown in.

- *Tabs* – another name for the front curtains.

- *Travellers* – two curtains that cross the stage.

If you *page* a curtain you hold it open for someone else to go through.

Session 19: Recording and Listening to Your Voice

INTRODUCTION

Historically people with learning disabilities had a small voice – they were not often encouraged to speak up for themselves. Thankfully this situation is now changing through the work of individuals and organisations such as People First.

You may well find a significant part of your vocal work is to encourage people to make a louder sound or to vocalise with more confidence. Recording voices and listening to them played back can be a useful way of developing the other vocal work that's been explored throughout the course. Hearing the recorded sound of your own voice can be liberating and magical, particularly for people with profound disabilities.

Recording has many uses in your work, and in this session we are offering various ideas which we have found particularly useful. Once again, two hours isn't long enough to use all these suggestions, but you will be able to pick the ones most appropriate to your students and project.

For our purposes, the uses of recording fall into two main categories:

1. Developing your voice.

2. Creating an artistic end product.

DEVELOPING YOUR VOICE

The sound of our own voice when recorded comes as quite a shock to everyone and it can take time to get used to hearing it. Given time and familiarity with this sound, as others hear it, we come to accept and hopefully admire it as part of the essence that makes up our individuality. If we hear things to be changed or developed we can then work on them even more easily. You'll find students enjoy listening to their voices and that the process helps them to analyse ways to improve volume and clarity. It can also be a pleasure for them to pick out their own voice on the tape when you have recorded more than one person.

1. Microphone Circle

Students in a circle. How you approach this exercise will really depend on the type of microphone at your disposal. The idea is to record each student's voice under the same conditions. A multidirectional mike can be placed in the centre of the circle. Anything more sophisticated and unidirectional will have to be carried round the circle by you.

First try a group rendition of anything familiar – say, 'Happy Birthday', or any vocal exercise that has become a favourite. Conduct the sound, first loud, then soft. Listen to the tape; let the students enjoy the group sound they've made.

Next, ask each person to record a short piece into the mike – it could be just his or her name. When each person has contributed, playback and listen.

2. Guess the Voice

From the above material, see who can recognise their own voice. Ask for any comments on vocal quality. What are the differences? Are there any voices that can't be heard? Most students will want to make some sort of impact on the tape, so ask those whose voices were faint to try again, this time making a louder sound.

Playback and listen. Is everyone pleased with the result? Can you all hear a difference? Finish off with a rousing chorus of something familiar.

3. Confidence and Clarity

Look back at *Session 14*. Try some of the exercises that encourage clarity and hear them back – for example, Away by the Shores of Far Brazil, any tongue twisters, any vowel repetitions adding consonants. Students who have trouble forming certain consonants may be able to work on them better having heard the differences on tape.

4. Accents and Finding a Voice

Use the tape recorder to explore the sound of different regional accents. What accents are present in the group? Where was everybody born? The recording will help to define the vowels and rhythms that identify the region. Talk about character work. Some of the characters in your performance project may adopt an accent – using the tape recorder to record examples could help students learn and copy new accents. Show them how to use the pause button so they can repeat phrases.

You may already have worked on the effects of changing the pitch of the voice to discuss age, authority, class. Listen to these differences on the tape recorder.

5. Chords

Harmonies – three students are given a note to sing or hum for a count of ten and the results are recorded individually on separate sources. They are then asked to repeat the same note together and make a harmony. Often this isn't quite managed. Hearing the chord played back on tape may make things clearer, as playing the notes on a piano would. Play with the tape – listen to them individually and then play all three notes from separate sources together.

6. Mike-Stand Presenting/PA

If you have access to a mike with PA, the amplification of students' voices can do wonders to build confidence.

Look back at *Session 2*. The students will have developed in confidence over the first 17 sessions. Try some of the self-presentation exercises using the mike-stand. Does the amplified sound of their voice change anything? Are students able to use the mike and look at the audience? Does it give them a sense of power, of being listened to?

A game to incorporate delivering a short piece to the mike could be *Lonely Hearts*. Students could present a three-line introduction to themselves in the manner of a 'small ad'. For example, 'John, 23, tall dark and handsome, good sense of humour, would like to meet girl for friendship and fun. Must like deep-sea diving!'

Another could be *Band Intros*. Each student thinks of an over-the-top way of introducing their favourite band at Glastonbury or Wembley

Stadium. For example, 'And now, presenting, for the only time this year in England, all the way from Iceland the one and only fantastically wonderful – Golden Gnomes!'

7. Recording Songs

Students will enjoy creating a 'record' of their singing skills. You can take the opportunity of exploring different musical genres by recording the same song in different ways – for example, Happy Birthday in a blues/reggae/ operatic/punk style. Ask students about their favourite singers and then to demonstrate what makes them special – it may be the Spice Girls' dancing or Elvis's vocal wobble. You may be able to make a 'compilation tape' of the various 'artists'. Of course, access to a karaoke machine unleashes all sorts of other possibilities!

The use of a tape recorder can be a good way of integrating someone who is not very verbal into a group song. That person may be able to press a button to play a pre-recorded harmony, or sound, to be incorporated into the song.

Vocal rounds can be created by using three different tape recorders, which three different people can switch on in time, or with the help of a conductor.

8. Walkmans

Personal stereos can be an invaluable tool for learning lines. Many professional actors use them particularly when learning a huge part or a play that has only two or three characters in it.

Many students have personal stereos to listen to their favourite music or talking books. They can be shown how to use them for learning lines. Students who can't read or who are visually impaired can have an equal chance of learning lines using the following method.

Students in a circle around a multidirectional microphone. Using the prepared script, place yourself behind the student and whisper their line, or section of the line. The student then repeats it loudly. You will have to move from student to student according to the demands of the script. If you have a sophisticated tape recorder you may be able to move from student to student using the 'pause' button to cover both your tracks and your whispers. This way, you will end up with a more fluent tape. When you have finished the whole play, make enough copies of the tape to give one to everyone. Each student will then have a copy of the play to listen to and will be able to learn lines from listening to their own voice.

For students with good reading skills another way to learn lines of a script with only a few characters is to record the whole play but leaving one character out. Leave gaps where that character speaks. The student playing that part is then able to listen to the tape, and speak their lines into the gaps.

9. Using the Technology

Learning how to use the different functions of the tape recorder – how to switch on the mike and position it correctly can be an empowering experience. Students can then use it for interviewing each other, making 'Dictaphone' messages, recording sound effects and wild-tracks. Students with more multiple and profound disabilities may be able to contribute by switching machines on and off and volumes up and down.

10. Interviewing on Tape

Students will have seen many news and celebrity interviews on television and heard them on the radio.

Fact finding/getting to know you – brainstorm questions for each interviewer to ask a partner. They could be questions about ordinary life, or the interviewee could take on a role of, say a favourite pop star. Then, working in pairs, record each interview, preferably with the interviewer working the tape recorder as well as asking the questions.

11. Sampler Boards

These are small hand-held keyboards/synthesisers available at good musical instrument stores. They are great for making sound effects and sound landscapes. They are particularly fun and effective in work with people with multiple and profound learning disabilities.

CREATING AN ARTISTIC END PRODUCT

Many of your students will listen to the radio, probably choosing music stations over others which offer drama. Now we are going to consider using tape and radio techniques both in drama and music format. Let's begin with looking at verbal drama.

Creating a drama piece on tape could be a good introduction to listening to plays or serials on, say, Radio 4. Students may also be familiar with talking books as another form of entertainment, particularly if reading is difficult. It can be particularly satisfying to work on taped dialogue as an artistic end product. You may want to record a section of a radio drama or soap, for example, *The Archers* to give them an idea, or play an extract from a talking book.

1. Six-minute Scene

Create a mini play with several characters that plays for six minutes. Brainstorm for ideas. This will be an improvised piece. Experiment with starting and stopping the tape as appropriate, using the erase function as an editing mechanism.

2. Soap Opera

Discuss favourite TV soaps. Choose the most popular. Discuss the difference between watching a scene and listening to a scene created through sound and dialogue. For example, if the scene is set in a pub – The Rovers Return, The Queen Vic, The Woolpack – think about sound effects, clinking glasses, ringing of till, drinking-up bell, doors opening and closing, juke-box playing in background, etc. Obviously this in itself could take up a complete session or several if you worked in detail. For example, you could go out and record your soap opera 'on location' or use props that are in the room, or bring in things from home.

3. News Bulletin

Students can make up 'local' news items about their lives, featuring support workers, day centre staff, family and issues which are of direct interest to them. You could provide a dramatic signature tune by recording directly off the radio or TV, or make up your own portentous jingle. This could be newsroom based, with a 'reader', but also include 'on location' reports from other people. The news items could also contain interviews.

4. Radio Commercials

Brainstorm for products to sell (see *Commercial Break* in Session 10). Play some examples from the radio to illustrate how short radio commercials are, and how the voice really must 'sell' the product. What is special about the voice? Talk about the use of energy, persuasiveness, friendliness, sexiness, different accents, etc. Usually radio commercials have jingles. You could make up your own using voices and or instruments.

5. Creation of a Soundtrack

Look back at *Soundtrack Story* and *Atmospherics* in Session 5. Using these as a starting point for inspiration, record your results – these could be for their own end, or you could use them as a background to your Six-minute Scene or Soap Opera, or as the beginnings of a soundtrack for your performance project.

6. Looking at Music

Most students will have a favourite pop star of the moment. Begin by talking about music on the radio and ask them to bring in favourite tapes, and to talk about why they like them. This could lead on to a *Desert Island Discs* idea.

7. Desert Island Discs

Ask everyone to bring in a favourite record, CD or tape. Try to encourage students not just to bring in their latest favourite, but to try and bring in an all-time favourite – something which has a personal resonance. Play these and then interview the students on the reasons for their choice, or they can work in pairs as 'interviewer' and 'guest' and record the results. For this exercise it is obviously necessary to have both playback and recording facilities on your machine. Your 'programme' will be a collection of reminiscences and songs from a number of different people rather than the traditional eight selections from one person.

8. Disc Jockeys

Find 'funky' styles to introduce a programme of music. Everyone will have their own ideas of what to include, so you'll inevitably have quite a few different styles. You could pre-record a selection of excerpts from different radio shows and stations including national, commercial and local. Listen to the DJs' personal styles and musical tastes. Perhaps create your own 'posse' – one main DJ with several sidekicks to contribute and laugh in the right places!

RELATING THE WORK TO PERFORMANCE THEMES

In *Romeo and Juliet*, five ideas to think about could be:

- choosing music for the ball
- a soundtrack for the whole piece
- scene change music
- news reports on the gang warfare between the rival families
- reporting the deaths.

In Holidays, five ideas to think about could be:

- travel programmes on radio
- travel commercials
- airport flight and gate announcements and information
- in-flight entertainment and captain and flight attendant announcements
- holiday destination/country soundtrack – tropical cicadas, frogs, waves, etc.

Session 20: Videoing and Watching Yourself

In the late twentieth century, television has become an inescapable presence in all our lives. It has replaced the fireplace as the focus of most of our living rooms, it has become the most popular source of news and information, it is the provider of improbable hours of home entertainment, and it has become a surrogate companion in many homes. As an education medium it has become commonplace not only in school but also in every possible venue: everywhere from a museum to an in-flight information service uses television and, increasingly, interactive video as an educational aid.

The actors, celebrities and presenters of television have become our heroes, familiars and villains. We admire them and we want to join them. We feel we know them and we think we can criticise them. Television is something that everybody has an opinion about, and more and more with the advent of cable and community television, phone-ins and audience contribution shows, it is something in which we all have the opportunity to participate.

You have the possibility of harnessing all of these aspects of television in your work with your students. If you have access to even rudimentary equipment you can work with them in the medium of video. They will inevitably be excited about seeing themselves on a screen; they will also be empowered by helping to create a programme idea and by having hands-on access to the technology.

Here are a few ideas which you may want to use in the future. Many projects could, of course, take a whole term. If you have only one or two sessions in which to use video equipment, we've suggested a few ideas for 'taster' sessions. You can also use video to demonstrate particular aspects of your project work, or you could use video in the actual theatre project to create a multimedia event.

1. Video Equipment

If you are working in a Further Education College or Day Centre make sure you book your equipment, usually from Media Resources or Facilities, well in advance. Some large colleges are lucky enough to have their own studio, but demands on its time are usually huge, so make sure you get your request in early, and arrive on the day well rehearsed.

It is not necessary to have 'state of the art' technology, but often the newer the equipment, the simpler it is to operate. If you have a colleague or friend who is available and is able to use a camera it is a good idea to have them operate for you as this will give you the freedom of working with the students without any added distractions. The basics:

- video camera – various types. Most have built-in microphones and some have built-in editing facilities, even the domestic ones such as those purchased in the High Street.
- film – depends which type of camera you have. We have used in the past VHS and Hi-8, but now use where possible DVC digital stock in a digital camera as it is easier to edit.
- tripod – for a steady picture.
- video player
- television or monitor.

If at all possible some time should be spent instructing some of your students in the operation of the equipment. For some, learning the technical side of filming will be a skill every bit as empowering as watching themselves perform on camera.

2. Visual Record

A source of great satisfaction and pride for the students is of course to have a physical record of their production/performance to take home and keep. Copying videotapes is, unfortunately quite expensive, so needs to be carefully budgeted for, or you could raise money from the students by individual subscription. A video is also a good record for you of their progress and your work.

3. Filming

When you are working on filming an event, episode or extract from your project you will be amazed at how long it will take, if you are tying to make it look in any way professional. Anything a little more ambitious than an overall covering (master) shot of a scene takes time. If you intend to edit, you will need at least the following shots:

- a master shot of each set up (section of scene covered by one camera position)
- a mid shot covering the important action or conversation, which includes the protagonists of the scene
- close-ups of the characters talking, and their reactions.

Even with these bare shots, you will need to repeat each piece of action/dialogue a minimum of four times for a two-character scene. Of course, in reality the number of takes will inevitably be far more than that, allowing for mistakes to be covered and choices to be made over the quality of each take.

It will require a great deal of discipline and patience from your students to allow this process to happen successfully, so it's not something to be undertaken with every group. However, even a video of blanket coverage of an event from a camera on a tripod, or selective shots using a hand-held camera, can be very satisfying as a record.

Should you be contemplating any outside location shooting you will probably need some assistance in making sure those that are not directly involved in the scene are catered for. You should also make sure you have spoken to, and obtained permission from, the owners of any locations that might feature in your scene.

4. Teaching Tool

All the way through the sessions you may find opportunities to incorporate the use of video into your exploration of various different aspects of theatre.

Simple exercises such as *Walking in Space* are enhanced by viewing them on video. Ask students to move around the room. You provide a commentary, bringing to their attention how they are moving, for example, 'become aware of your shoulders. Are they tense? Are they raised? Try to relax your shoulders as you move around the room.'

It could be particularly useful to repeat some of the exercises of the early sessions on building self-confidence and presentation (see Session 2 and Session 3). The video will show the students how their self-confidence has increased and they should enjoy a simple demonstration of performance on video.

Simply asking students to *walk* across the stage/room illustrates aspects of everyone's different physical personality, which you can all observe on video.

What is conveyed about their attitude in that simple walk? Does one student stare consistently at the floor? Does another find it impossible to look away from the camera? Is a third reluctant to move at all? What does their posture tell them and you about their confidence and relationship with their own physicality? Perhaps seeing these things played back will help each one to try again. We all want to look our best on camera!

Carrying on from this, give the students characters in their *journey* across the stage, for example, an old man carrying a heavy load, a child skipping to grandma's house, a spy covering her tracks, a servant bowing out backwards. Individual characters from your possible themes could develop from this exercise.

Work around emotions, as discussed in Session 17, could be developed by using the camera in close-up to look at how people's faces change when they are feeling different emotions. The *Oh Game* from Session 8 could be useful here.

Performance size could well be demonstrated on video. Students whose work is small and quiet will see that this can be a positive quality on camera. Students who tend towards the over-loud and boisterous will see how this can be inappropriate.

5. Taster Days

INTERVIEWS

Use the video to record interviews. Either take on the role of interviewer yourself, or ask the students to interview each other. There are a number of different formats for conducting interviews.

- The interviewer is behind/operating the camera in a documentary/ *cinéma-vérité* 'Molly Dineen – *The Ark* sort of way.
- The interview could take place in the traditional 'sofa' configuration of breakfast television.
- The interviewer is behind a desk, the interviewee to the right.
- The standing interviewer holds a microphone in the manner of a news reporter.
- There is no apparent interviewer – the student is answering prepared questions from an out of shot source.

Any number of subjects suggest themselves:

- asking for personal history or reminiscence
- vox pop on issues of daily life – transport, college facilities, the day centre, etc.
- current affairs
- tastes – music and film preferences, etc.

CHAT SHOWS

Set up an audience/studio situation in the manner of a non-celebrity chat show. Decide on a topic for discussion/scrutiny. It could be a serious topical debate around personal issues of the group's life, or you could simulate one of the more outrageous subjects often featured on this sort of show. Students can take it in turn to be guest and the audience can ask questions via the 'host' (possibly you). A number of students can take their turn on stage in the discussion, joining the initial 'guest' to add their opinions in the manner of programmes such as the *Ricki Lake Show*. Cheers and whoops can add to the fun. The playback of a show like this immediately features everyone on camera at some point.

NEWS READING

As a group, script a news bulletin. For added authenticity, pre-record portentous music for the introduction. Decide on the style of presentation. Is it *Six O'Clock News* or *Newsround*? Set up a suitable 'studio' space.

Will you have a weather report? Using a flip chart and magic markers, create a weather map, or two groups could create one each, for today and tomorrow. Film the results.

Do we expect our news to have a certain solemnity of delivery? Could the readers keep a straight face? Did they manage to focus on the camera if they were improvising the report? If they were reading, how easy was it to also look up at the camera/audience? A trip to the MOMI museum in London, or Granada studios in Manchester allows people to have a go at news reading using auto-cue, should you have time/facilities for organising trips.

ADVERTS AGAIN

Bring in real products or invent fantasy ones – 'the sludge-de-gulper' for unblocking drains, for example.

Using the discipline of a very short time slot for an advert (try two minutes rather than thirty seconds!) devise an advert in groups of three.

IDEAS FOR FURTHER LONG-TERM PROJECT WORK

As we've said, work on video could be a whole different course that could take up a whole term or even year of work. We know of a group who've created their own episode of *The Bill* lasting approximately 20 minutes. It was filmed in and around their day centre in Battersea. A day centre-based group in the West Midlands specialises in making training films, and films that raise awareness of issues affecting learning disabled people for use in the wider community. Projects like these may well need their own funding and sponsorship, as equipment hire and professional expertise should be paid for. Nevertheless, they are hugely worth the effort as the end result is immensely satisfying for the participants, and very informative for everyone who sees such high quality work.

Awareness Issues

Your group, particularly if they have been attending a 'Speak for Yourself', or self-advocacy class, may want to produce a documentary style video highlighting an issue important in their own lives. This could combine techniques of pieces to camera, with location work and interviews.

Prospectus

If you are based at a college, you and your group may want to make a film illustrating your work there. Most Further Education Colleges offer a number of different courses for learning disabled people. Your film could be a video prospectus for the college to show at local day centres, etc. to encourage further participation and learning at college.

Drama

As we all know, the possibilities of film are endless. But a simplified version of a well-known television series such as *The Bill* maintains interest over a long period of time. As with a theatre piece, you must tailor your own dramatic projects to the inspiration and ability of your group.

PART III

Working Towards a Performance or Showing of Work

SINGING WITH A TAPE RECORDER

Michael Hehy

Romeo and Juliet[1]

Introduction to the Group

Paddington Arts is a building-based organisation which works predominantly with youth groups who are under-represented in mainstream community provision. The Drama Group for People with Learning Disabilities on a Saturday morning is an independent group of 18 students between the ages of 16 and 29.

The students are Isobel, Catherine, Sarah, Shanti, Frances, Sima, Christine, Gordon, Tim B, Paul, Tom W, Derrick, Richard, Lester, Julian, Wilson, Pittin and Nila. The students all have an interest in acting and have chosen to attend, some with great encouragement from their parents. The group are all physically mobile except Tom W who has limited mobility and uses sticks. During the session he likes to work on a swivel office chair on wheels which gets him about. Some students have quite challenging behaviour, in particular Paul, Tim B, Wilson and Sima.

The sessions run weekly on a Saturday morning from 11am to 1pm with a stop for a teabreak mid-session. This is very important as it provides an opportunity for the group to mix together and to practise social skills. The tea break can often be half an hour in length and is roughly taken from 12 midday to half past. Often during the break, the work is discussed along with everyday goings on in their lives.

Five support workers attend the group: Alan, Tim K, Patti, Mandy and Sophie who cover alternate weeks and join in enthusiastically, as do Virginia, Sarah's mother and Joan, Catherine's mother. With such a large group it is good to have so much support although ironically sometimes it turned out that the support was almost too enthusiastic, occasionally threatening to take over a scene!

---

1   A project devised with Paddington Arts.

For this section of the book we feel it is more appropriate to describe the work in terms of how each scene evolved rather than dividing it into sessions as in 'Holidays'. Most people will have an idea of the story of *Romeo and Juliet* and will readily be able to identify the sources.

The group is ongoing and as it has been meeting for approximately two years certain relationships have been developed, along with an immense group trust and support. This has led to useful short cuts in working methods; not having to explain everything in detail every time you repeat a building block exercise or development work on improvisation.

Whilst waiting for the group to assemble, we begin by sitting in a circle. Often the group is haphazard in its arrival – sometimes it can take up to half an hour for the whole group to get together. Some students arrive en masse from another weekend activity group for people with learning disabilities which provides them with transport. Others are independent travellers and arrive on their own. The remaining students are brought by family members.

As we wait for students to arrive we have a general chat with those present about their week and how they are feeling. These students usually help to set up and organise the room – putting chairs in a circle, etc. Once everyone has arrived we generally sit in a circle and quickly go round saying One word about how we are *feeling* that morning at that time. At the end of the session we repeat the same exercise to see if feelings have changed. Usually those who had felt down, low or not sure feel more positively about things.

This particular project began after an Easter break. Our first new session had to start with a general chat and discussion about *behaviour*, as a few personal crises and confrontations had been developing, and they had to be sorted out if everyone was to feel comfortable proceeding within the group structure.

Wilson in particular was a problem last term. He has a mild learning disability and is an only child of very busy working parents. We felt that he was really only coming to drama as 'something to do', and perhaps wasn't personally committed.

Paul, another student with learning disabilities and severe behavioural problems who had been quite violent in the previous term, was under very close supervision from Tim K, one of the larger male care workers. Paul is a man in his early twenties who is extremely large, very strong and prone to violent outbursts.

Tim B had been particularly disruptive last term and we needed to make sure that patterns of behaviour wouldn't repeat themselves. To this end we made sure that everyone wanted to proceed with the drama sessions and several students made a *verbal contract* in front of the whole group. The contract agreed was that anybody who was disruptive would then be suspended for the rest of the term. The group decided that this was the best plan of action to take.

When we are ready to start we begin with a physical warm-up. This can be a game, or physical and vocal exercises which are often led from week to week by individual students.

The Choice Of Theme

In the *theme discussion* sessions a definite desire to work on something romantic emerged that would also contain action and perhaps some conflict.

We talked about various boyfriend/girlfriend private situations. Some people talked about their own loved ones, some talked about the fact they would like a partner, and how their parents felt about that and why.

We improvised telling Mum/Dad about a new partner and acted out their reactions, both positive and negative. This led us to mention the story of *Romeo and Juliet* and how their parents were desperate to keep the families apart. This led on to further discussion and improvisation around where we might find groups of people quarrelling and fundamental issues of race, religion, class, etc. and how these things can escalate into gang situations and, ultimately, wars.

The family situation in the play led on to discussion and improvisation around arranged marriage. We learned a lot from several of the students from ethnic backgrounds who were more familiar with this practice. We discussed how Juliet might have felt about Paris even if she had never met Romeo.

We decided that the story of *Romeo and Juliet* would be a good structure on which to base our own project. We knew we only had 10 sessions until the Summer Break, and so decided to be flexible about the amount of the original story we could cover in that time. The important incidents to include, we all decided, were the Ball, the fight and the relationship with Mum and Dad. Everything and anything else could evolve.

We had a session on *storyboarding* in which individuals came up with pictures of gangs, a disco, a market place, a gym, Juliet's grave, etc.

Background Research

Around the time of working on this project, the film version of *Romeo and Juliet*, directed by Baz Lurhman, starring Leonardo di Caprio and Claire Danes was released. We organised a trip to the cinema which was highly inspirational for the whole group, both from the point of view of being excited by the film/play and the clarity of the storytelling, and in terms of bonding the group in a social activity.

Music

We also hired a video of *West Side Story* and showed extracts to contrast and compare. This led on to an exploration of the music we could use, and resulted in a session on dance for the project, using the Bernstein music, the soundtrack from the Baz Lurhman film and the Prokofiev ballet music.

Stage Fighting

Our session on movement led on to an exploration of stage fighting using swords (see Session 16 and below). It took almost a whole session to choreograph simple controlled sequences of lunges and parries. The warm-up consisted of a great deal of stretching and pliés and moving backwards without looking. We divided the group into pairs and one half advanced on the other who retreated while maintaining eye contact. Having mastered this, the pairs were then able to progress across the stage 'fighting' and avoiding others.

Swords And Masks

Having established that we wanted to use swords in a street brawl scene and masks at a ball, we devoted a session to prop making. The swords were rolled up newspapers stuck with sellotape and the creation of the masks turned into an individual project that was undertaken as an outside craft session organised by another group.

The Playing Area

Our studio is a large bright room which allowed for a 20 × 20 feet playing area, playing end on, with the audience in front. For furniture, we used two tables for the market stalls and three chairs. The tables were joined together across the stage to make the dining table in Scene Two, and the chairs placed one either end and one centre, to make a very 'posh' table.

The Capulets always entered from the Right, the Montagues from the Left. On two Saturdays when we weren't available to run the sessions, the students worked with a visiting Visual Artist and created a stunning backdrop to the action.

Storyboard/Captions

Sima, a group member with behavioural problems who came every week but who would often do her 'own thing' in the corner of the room, unless the activity involved dancing, was greatly interested in art. It had been Sima who had led the drawings on the initial *Storyboard scene pictures*. Sima decided that it would be a good idea to make up Scene Titles – to write them down on sheets – and to draw around them.

Narrator

We then considered that not all our audience would be able to read the cards, so it was decided that perhaps someone should also verbally introduce the scenes. Isobel volunteered to be the narrator and learned a sentence or a working title for each scene. Eventually we hit upon the idea of giving her a music cue for each introduction, which was some Prokofiev. Isobel decided to hold up the scene card that Sima had made as she spoke. It was a bit like the captions at a music hall or in a silent film.

Visual Cues

As we worked, we realised how difficult it was for many students to remember the sequence of events within a scene. Obviously the narrator and cards would help the scene-to-scene sequence, but we had to find a way of helping people remember cues. We hit upon a system of creating a big physical action as a catalyst to the next event or sometimes a *Freeze* served the same purpose. For example when the Montagues and Capulets are fighting in the market-place, different things happened during different rehearsals. We decided that the cue for The Prince of Verona to enter and break up the fight would be when Frances, who is a very reliable student, started to clap her hands and jump up and down. At the point in the dance where Romeo and Juliet first meet and speak to each other everyone else froze when a bell chimed.

SCENE ONE: THE MARKET-PLACE

Working from the structure of the original play the first Montague/ Capulet confrontation took place in 'a public place', here a street market.

After discussion about what could be sold, we decided that as we were going to use masks in the ball/party scene and swords to fight with, we would have two market stalls – one selling masks and hats, the other selling swords. As already described, these had been made in previous sessions.

We decided that support workers Sophie and Tim K would be the market sellers. They would be a Montague and Capulet respectively.

We split up the rest of the group into two halves – Montagues and Capulets – and they went to opposite sides of the 'playing area', to make entrances from the wings.

The two market sellers entered and began calling out improvised lines to sell their wares, for example, 'get your lovely party masks here – only £1', 'swords, sharp swords, killer swords, get them now – only £5'.

Slowly the students entered from their respective wing areas and began to mingle. We had spent time in our session on *Style* on greetings – in this case posh old fashioned greetings such as bowing and curtseying, using arms when bowing, etc. (see Session 16). A Montague only greeted a Montague and a Capulet only acknowledged a Capulet. If a Capulet met a Montague they looked daggers at each other (see Session 3). They had to appear to be physical with each other but had to avoid actual contact. This involved them circling each other, making aggressive gestures and faces, etc. During the above we played some more of the Prokofiev music as a prelude.

In improvising a market scene Tim B and Pittin (Capulets) stole from Sophie's (Montagues) stall. We decided that this worked and that we would keep it in. Once a fracas was well underway we decided to freeze the action at the point where a drum was struck from offstage. This became a cue for Derrick to proceed with his line 'Take that you Montague!' to Shanti, whilst biting his thumb at her in line with the Shakespearean insult, which had captured his fancy rather than any of the more modern insults/gestures that other people suggested!

This fight carried on, now using their swords as weapons, until Shanti fell down dead – another cue point. The groups then separated back to their respective sides of the playing area and started confronting each other by advancing forwards and backwards to each other using the chants they'd worked on in a previous vocal session (see Session 14).

The chants were *'Capulets stink'*, *'Dirty rotten montagues'*.

Gordon entered as The Prince of Verona, and broke up the 'fight' chanting. He had an improvised sentence along the lines of 'If anyone fights again they will be banished. Off you all go.'

Everyone played scared of The Prince who was the leader of the land (see Session 15 on *Status*). They bowed or curtseyed as they left the playing area – retreating to their respective 'wing' sides bowing backwards, etc.

SCENE TWO: JULIET'S PARENTS HAVING DINNER

We had talked about both Romeo's and Juliet's parents being rich, so to show this we created the Capulets' long, grand dining table and Tim W came up with the idea that they should have servants. (see Session 15). We decided that in this scene we would have Tim W playing Juliet's dad, Lord Capulet. Juliet's mum, Lady Capulet, was played by Isobel, and Juliet was played by Catherine.

Catherine is someone who has an unspecified learning disability. She has educational special needs but also has behaviour problems which manifest themselves into crises of confidence which become obsessional. We and the group always feel fantastic when Catherine takes a more prominent role. For her to come to the sessions takes a great deal of effort from both her and her mother.

Tim W decided it would be good if he and Isobel made a grand entrance to show exactly who they were. So we began the scene with the waiter or butler played by Shanti – nobody could decide if it was better for Shanti to be called waiter or butler, in the end we went with waiter as Shanti identified with that more easily – attending the table awaiting her 'bosses'.

Tim W told Shanti to hold out the chairs for them to sit on – he had seen this being done on television where people had servants to wait on them.

Catherine/Juliet was late for her dinner so after much calling from Tim W, Shanti was sent to bring her on stage 'down from her room' (see Session 17 – *Where Have I Come From/Where am I Going?*), where she was apparently playing CDs.

There were huge anachronisms in the final showing of work regarding time and period but it didn't matter at all.

Catherine arrived and played being in a bad mood. In one of the previous sessions we had talked about how teenagers often don't get on with their parents so the beginning of this scene came from that. Improvisation/status, teenagers/parents.

Frozen Pictures, a game similar to *Emotional Statues* or *Photographs* (see Section 8: *Feelings.*) in the first term had often involved restaurants and café scenes. The next part of this scene involved the 'ordering' of what the Capulet family wanted for their dinner which took Shanti on trips back and forth to a kitchen which was set up at one side of the playing area.

In the kitchen was Tim B as Cook and Pittin as Cook's helper. Shanti would take the order and mime writing it down. She would then go to the kitchen with the order and Tim B would invariably say that the food was 'off'. Shanti would then have to go back for a re-order. If this happened too many times, as a fail-safe Tim W/Lord Capulet would go to the kitchen and tell Cook that he and his helper were sacked.

We spent much time getting Tim B to understand that if he was sacked then that was that, as he had the lower status. Eventually after much practice he began to understand that he had to improvise asking for his job back. In rehearsal this part of the scene often went on too long and we would have to interrupt to get it back on course.

Eventually the food was set on the table, which was the cue for Tim W/Lord Capulet to talk about the party they were having for Catherine/Juliet, and to tell her about the arranged marriage with Paris.

Whilst they were eating, Tim W introduced the idea of Catherine marrying Paris, whom they had invited to the party. We had already improvised around the idea of an arranged marriage. Catherine decided initially that she was having none of it but was eventually persuaded at least to look at him. During this discussion, Lady Capulet wanted to know if he had any money – he has, he's loaded apparently so that is in his favour. Is money more important than feelings? Another issue that had come up.

Lady Capulet begins to choke on something – she says the food is bad; she calls the cook and assistant and sacks them once and for all.

Juliet goes mad and has a tantrum when she thinks about what her parents are suggesting, she also thinks it's terrible the way they are treating the servants. She gets in a real strop and walks out. Lord Capulet then has a go at Lady Capulet and says this is all her fault. Shanti goes and gets Juliet back. Mum apologises to dad and they all agree that they will see what happens at the party.

All these ideas and responses emerged whilst running the scene in improvisations, and most of what is described came from the actors themselves, with help and suggestions at rehearsal from ourselves, and the other students watching. As the sessions and rehearsals progressed, we felt strongly that the students should own their own work and be involved in the unfolding direction of the story.

SCENE THREE: MONTAGUES IN A BAR TALKING ABOUT GATECRASHING

One table was struck and the other moved Stage Right by Richard and Lester.

This scene grew from an improvisation about gatecrashing a friend's party which everyone in the group identified with. For the purposes of Romeo and Juliet we simply translated this to the party/ball.

The students suggested setting the scene in a pub. Isobel played the barmaid. Tim W played Romeo and Sophie (care worker) would play the bar landlady, Sarah and Shanti would play Romeo's friends.

Smoking was an issue for the group. Some group members wanted to smoke at break. The building was non-smoking. This scene was in essence about how they felt about smoking. Tim W/Romeo and Shanti/Friend started smoking in the pub which was a no-smoking pub. Isobel as barmaid insisted they extinguish their cigarettes – they refused – an argument ensued.

After much wrangling, the drinkers put out their cigarettes which was the cue to begin to talk about what they were going to do that night. They decided it was a Saturday night, which meant that nobody wanted to stay in.

Tim W/Romeo talked about the Capulet party and suggested they should gatecrash. It was a 'masked' or fancy dress party so no one would recognise them. If anyone did recognise them, they realised they would be thrown out and that there would probably be a fight. The decision to get their masks was the cue to exit. Isobel was left to clean up (and strike) her pub with the assistance of Richard and Lester.

SCENE FOUR: BOYS IN THE GYM WORKING OUT BEFORE PARTY

This scene essentially came out of an inspired warm-up session. We brought in the Bernstein *West Side Story* soundtrack and used it one day as a background to a *warm-up circle* where each student led a warm-up movement.

The *gym* track inspired some of the students to pretend they were at the gym and led us in mimed weightlifting exercises. From this idea, the students thought it would be interesting to have a scene set in a gym, where people were working out. We talked about different hobbies and discussed whether men and women always enjoy the same ones. At the Day Centre which some of the students attend during the week, there are separate groups for men and women. Although we all thought that portraying men working out in the gym juxtaposed with the scene which was to follow – girls putting on make-up – was horribly sexist and stereotypical, we and the students felt that it was sufficiently 'tongue in cheek' to be funny and not offensive.

To make the gym interesting we made four 'stations' where different activities took place – press-ups, sit-ups, dumb-bell weights, rowing, etc.

Julian decided he wanted to be the instructor. The men were then split into four groups – each assigned an initial station – and at points in the music Julian would blow on a whistle and everyone would move round one station. To mark the different stations we used the furniture that was at the back of the set. Chairs and upturned tables, and tables sitting on their end were used to represent gym equipment.

All the men enjoyed this scene immensely and it was a real chance to 'show off' in an acceptable way.

SCENE FIVE: GIRLS PUTTING ON MAKE-UP FOR PARTY

This scene developed as a response to the initial warm-up session which resulted in Scene four. It was quite a simple and effective scene which required very little rehearsal. We put the four tables in a row, with a row of chairs behind them – one for each of the women – to represent a very long dressing table. The women sat behind the desks on the chairs facing the audience (downstage; see Session 18) as if they were looking into a dressing table mirror.

We used the track *I Feel Pretty* from Bernstein's *West Side Story*. The women explored all the different things you might do when making up – miming putting on lipstick, mascara, hairspray, jewellery, painting nails, etc. and sharing things with the women sitting next to them.

Often learning disabled women are not socially encouraged to wear make-up, so as a dramatic exercise, for some of them this was particularly liberating – a celebration of beauty almost.

At a certain point in the music, the girls got up from the table, picked up a chair as if it was a dancing partner, i.e. waltz position, and danced around the table from stage left to stage right twice (see Session 18), until they were back in their original position. This represented them practising dancing for the party.

To fill the music that was left, Catherine came up with the idea of dancing on top of the tables which looked really good – but only after we made sure that the tables were really secure and that the women dancing on the tables were people with good balance, who had no problems with heights.

The subject matter of *Romeo and Juliet* brought up in discussion and in practical work expressions of emotion and feelings of a personal nature, and related to sexuality. Often learning disabled people are not given the opportunity to express themselves sexually and we have found that great sensitivity is needed when dealing with these issues. In particular we have found that when taking on the roles of boyfriends and girlfriends, learning disabled people often take more time to de-role and find it more difficult to separate play acting from reality. Make sure you feel confident in dealing with such situations. It is important to know who else to contact, i.e. keyworkers or counsellors, if you feel you are unsuitably qualified to deal with a particularly sensitive situation.

SCENE SIX: GUESTS ARRIVE AND ARE ANNOUNCED

We often used to rehearse this scene prior to tea break, because of the location of the kitchen. We would exit 'two by two' from the main studio and progress down the corridor. At the entrance to the kitchen, we would have Richard as the Master of Ceremonies announcing the couples, names loudly to Tim W and Sarah, playing Lord and Lady Capulet.

In the actual performance, we set back the tables, formed a long line of couples who would progress across the playing area to stage right where the Master of Ceremonies would announce who they were to the Capulets – Lord, Lady and Juliet. People had great fun making up silly titles for themselves, Lord and Lady Muck, Sir Scratch Card and Lady Lottery, etc. Once they had been introduced and either kissed Lady Capulet's hand or shaken hands, they went back across the stage to mingle with the other guests. Whenever two people met they would bow or curtsey.

Props used for this were swords, masks and fans – as before. Music used – *Arrival of the Guests* from Prokofiev's *Romeo and Juliet.*

Again there was a cue, so that everyone would know what to do next or what to move on to. Once everyone had been introduced it was Richard as MC who gave the cue, which was the announcement 'Let the dancing commence!'

SCENE SEVEN: BALL DANCE; ROMEO MEETS JULIET

The group wanted to make up a dance which would look impressive. The dance we ended up with was really quite sophisticated and had been used as an extension of a warm-up throughout the term – each week building on a new section. We decided that at the end of the dance Romeo should meet Juliet. In this scene Derrick played Romeo and Isobel played Juliet.

Everyone had a partner – it didn't matter what the make-up of the couple was, i.e. same sex. Couples were paired so that there was at least one strong link in the partnership who could cope if things went slightly wrong.

We had eight couples facing opposite each other in two lines of four, making two separate groups:

A	A A	A
A	A A	A
A	A A	A
A	A A	A

Music used: *Dance of the Knights* from Prokofiev's *Romeo and Juliet*
The basic steps were as follows:

1. Bow/curtsey

2. Hold hands in circle, round for 8, back for 8

3. Right hands to middle, round for 8

4. Left hands to middle, round for 8

5. Two lines facing partner – bending knee with each step, across and back, 8 steps across, 8 steps back

6. Two lines opposite partner – advance to middle (do-se-do) go back

7. Four pas de bas

8. Figures of 8 in straight lines (fours) until back in place

9. Four pas de bas

10. In to middle, twirl partner once

11. Back in line curtsey/bow.

The end step, No 11 was the cue for everyone to *freeze*. This was the cue for Romeo and Juliet to stare at each other – walk towards each other – everyone else still frozen – circle each other holding palms to palms as in Shakespeare and the films we had watched.

After they had completed two circles it was Gordon's cue to say 'Take that you Montague' to Sarah with biting thumb gesture as in Scene one.

This was the cue to move to the next scene.

SCENE EIGHT: FIGHT AT BALL

This was more or less a repetition of the opening fight which was stopped by Tim W as Lord Capulet. Romeo and his friends had their masks taken off and were thrown out.

SCENE NINE: BALCONY SCENE

Derrick stayed as Romeo. Isobel stood on box behind an upturned desk to represent the balcony. Both had learned these lines during the term.

Isobel: 'Romeo, Romeo, wherefore art thou Romeo?'

Derrick: 'She speaks, Oh speak again bright angel!'

This was as far as we got with the work, so we decided that we would call the showing of work 'Nine scenes from Romeo and Juliet'. It felt irrelevant that the story was not completed as it stood alone as a whole and worked as it was.

On the day of the show, everyone was highly nervous about performing in front of an invited audience of peers, family and friends, but all rose to the challenge and were so proud of what they had achieved and how much everyone enjoyed their work.

Holidays[1]

SESSION ONE

This was a group of nine with two care workers who had been meeting regularly and were working well. However there was scarcely a week when all nine arrived together. After two terms' work we then had eight weeks potentially to create a piece to show. We felt it was most appropriate for the theme and sessions to be student led, so ideas flowed and progressed from week to week directly from student input and improvisations.

We talked through possible themes for an end showing of work which was intended to be seen by prospective new students for the following year's work at a Further Education College.

These sessions began after the spring break. We'd all had quite a good time, many people had been away or were excited about possible summer holidays.

We came up with the umbrella title 'Holidays', knowing that everyone had some experience of going away and could contribute ideas or fantasies.

To wake ourselves up physically we began the session with a physical game which has some relevance to journeys (*Crossing the River* Session 4).

We continued by adapting *My Grandmother went to Market* from Session 7 and calling it *I Went On Holiday and I Packed*.

We sat down in a circle and brainstormed specific ideas and personal reminiscences for a holiday theme. What did people want from a holiday? Various typical responses were 'sea and a rest', 'a change', 'something different'. Rommel, who is not normally very verbally forthcoming, and for whom anyway English is a second language suddenly became very

[1]   Regent's Park Centre, Kingsway College, London. Further Education Course In Drama for Adults with Learning Disabilities

excited and we discovered eventually that he was describing a family reunion in Bangladesh.

We wrote ideas on a flip chart:

- caravan in Wales
- adventure holiday from group home – to include backpacking and abseiling
- coach trip
- family reunion
- safari
- New York
- by the sea.

                                                    TEA BREAK

The Journey

For many people the mode of transport was very important. Everyone had a lot of experiences of buses and coaches, most people had been on a plane, and quite a few had been on the ferry to France or the Isle of Wight.

We divided into two groups and chose our own method of transport to improvise, which were a plane and a coach. There is never any shortage of drivers! The task was to create something in two groups of four that could move independently but in unison around the room.

The *plane* had a pilot, holding on to a steering wheel, two people as central wings who linked arms over the shoulder and held out their other arms, and a tail who was Kwouk Seng, someone who prefers always to follow rather than initiate. Together they managed to move slowly around the room, although the tail had to be encouraged to keep up!

The *coach* had a driver, Philippa in her wheelchair and three passengers all sitting on chairs. Somehow they managed to lift their chairs in a crouched position and progress around the room while singing a variation of 'Summer Holiday'.

Holiday Statues

Using ideas from the Holiday experiences we'd discussed we created a version of *Musical statues*. This was to give instant mimed pictures or images of holidays without any forethought or discussion. We asked people to move around the room and when the music stopped we would give a command which they could use to create any image that came to mind, in any way. (You could be creative in making a tape which would also suggest ideas with different moods and tempi or even use current holiday favourites – that year it was the Macarena.)

Some suggestions for Musical statues:

- sightseeing
- skyscraper
- looking at wildlife through binoculars
- hot
- cold
- swimmer
- winter sport
- rock climbing
- shells
- Disneyland.

As always it was interesting to see who created independently and who had to look to others to copy. Every so often we would ask everyone to look at someone's particularly inspired statue. We encouraged everyone to use their whole bodies and faces in each 'snapshot'.

The session ended with further discussion of how the term would progress. We emphasised the need to really listen and remember what we did from week to week. Many of the things we would be working on now we would come back to again and again in rehearsal. We asked people to bring holiday photos, brochures, etc. for next time.

Throughout the session Philippa had been very vocally disruptive. She had been coming to the class for two years, and although she is not very verbally skilled, we were pretty certain she enjoyed the classes. She was showing unhappiness with something by making very loud, repetitive noises, which other members of the class found disturbing. We and they asked her what the problem was, and to stop being disruptive, as we found it difficult to concentrate with that noise. She did stop for a while but then began again. At the end of the class we had to make it clear to her and to her care worker that this behaviour was not acceptable in college, and hope that the problem, what ever it was, would be explored at home before next week.

SESSION TWO
Warm-Up

In pairs decide on a part of the body to warm up and then demonstrate to the rest of the class for everyone to copy. By this time we had discovered which combinations of people worked well together. Some people had to concentrate on not giggling, for others eye contact was the most important focus of pair work. We went round the pairs encouraging people to make bigger stretches or help each other to balance, whatever was appropriate.

We recapped the work from last week. Had anyone brought pictures? There were some snaps, pictures of sun, sea, coaches, planes, desert and some brochures from Disneyland. Everyone agreed that they would like to include an element of Disneyland into the final piece.

Today's task was to decide *Who* was going on holiday. Ideas were:

- family
- group of Friends
- Honeymoon couple.

We split into three groups. A pair and two threesomes with a teacher or carer in each, and allocated the combinations of holiday-makers. The task was to decide where each was going and then make a scene.

- The family was dad, gran and two kids. They went to Wales in a caravan.
- The group of Friends went to an activity centre and put on their rucksacks and went hiking.
- The Honeymoon Couple went in a car and on to a Ferry.

In the family group Rommel obviously enjoyed his role of authority as dad, and enjoyed telling the children off.

The Friends were led by Tom, who had recently been on such a holiday and knew exactly what to pack. Philippa obviously enjoyed being led by Tom, she became quieter and looked at him out of the corner of her eyes.

The Honeymoon Couple, Graham and Mary, liked their title but were very reluctant even to hold hands. Graham has problems with balance and was using Mary's hand to steady himself. Mary felt the pressure on her hand was too great. We worked on Graham relaxing his grip by keeping his weight down and in contact with the floor, and repeated clenching and unclenching hand relaxation moves. When they sat on the Ferry the couple began a dialogue about their trip. Physical difficulties were resolved and verbally each agreed with everything the other said!

 TEA BREAK

After tea we talked about the three improvisations, and discussed future casting. It was decided that focusing on the Honeymoon Couple and their trip would leave everyone else free to be other characters that the couple could encounter.

So the next task is Scene One – The Honeymoon Couple board the ferry.

We played *Captain's Coming* (Session 5) to remind ourselves of the size and shape of a ship. We broke down the essentials of a ferry and decided it needed

- a Captain
- two Sailors
- a Bar
- Cars
- a Bow Door
- a Gangplank.

Benny, who is good at mime but has limited vocal skills, became the Captain. He gave himself a steering wheel, a peaked cap and a pair of binoculars, and positioned himself 'Forward'. Jennifer, a carer, and Kwouk Seng became the Cars. Tom who is very tall was the Bow Doors by raising and lowering his arms, 'Aft'. Gary who is very enthusiastic, excitable and finds concentration very hard was a sailor, with Rommel. Philippa tended the bar in the middle of the stage. The gangplank was two chairs down stage centre and the Honeymoon Couple entered from the Audience.

The initial improvisation had only two instructions. First the cars must enter through the Bow Door, and then the Foot Passengers (the Honeymoon Couple) could enter via the gangplank. Everyone must find some reason to use the Bar.

The initial improvisation was very chaotic but dramatic! Mary and Graham entered via the gangplank but then Mary jumped overboard. Everybody except her husband rushed to help! The Captain took her to the bar for a reviving drink, and she thanked him for saving her. So the essence of the scene was created. The future task would be to refine it and remember it from week to week.

We ended the session by recapping everyone's roles in this scene, asking them to remember what had happened and think of a destination for the Honeymoon Couple for the next week.

Philippa's disruption continued this week, and escalated into the canteen at tea break, causing annoyance to the other users. More talking didn't help, the only thing that seemed to distract her from her problem was fast physical activity, and constant attention, which of course was not practical all the time. We spoke to her carer and contacted her keyworker and were invited to her upcoming client review to see if together we could sort it out.

SESSION THREE
Warm-Up

Simon Says. One student stands with their back to the others and demonstrates a now familiar physical warm-up move, also explaining it where possible with words, for example, 'Simon says...stretch up to the ceiling'. The others copy. It is a good discipline and concentration exercise to remain facing away from everyone else, and for the others to work out how to do the movement by copying a back view rather than the familiar front view.

First Rehearsal

We asked students to recap verbally the ferry scene. Who played what? Most people remembered vividly what had happened. This time we would break down slowly the individual elements of the scene. We told everyone to be patient if they were waiting to work on their own 'moment'.

We started with the Cars. Kwouk Seng began to easily follow Jennifer's lead. After reaching the Bow Doors we coached 'Park the car and get out' and were delighted when he copied pulling up the handbrake and even more when he initiated opening the car door himself. We rehearsed these actions several times. Tom had no problem with his 'Bow Doors' and invented a noise for them.

We then turned to the Honeymoon Couple. What would happen if Mary did fall off the gangplank? Surely her *husband* would do something? What would Graham say? 'Help help!'? Can Mary swim? She decided yes and began the breaststroke, also calling for help. The *Sailors* who had been standing to attention by the gangplank ran to tell the Captain. Gary decided he would say 'Mary has fallen in, what shall we do?' He kept saying he couldn't remember the line, and would close his eyes and strike his head in frustration. Really it was excitement that was getting the better of him, not his memory. We got him on his own, made him open his eyes and take deep breaths and deliver the line calmly, which pretty quickly he managed to do.

The Captain sprang into action. He saluted the sailors, picked something off the wall and ran to Mary. He threw the object overboard and we realised it was a rope ladder. Mary began to climb up it magnificently. How would they achieve the last scramble on to the deck? Benny took Mary's hands and she jumped aboard.

Everyone turned for applause. But surely the scene hadn't ended yet? Where would they take Mary? Was she all right? Was there anyone on board who hadn't yet been involved in the scene? It was decided that she should be taken to the Bar.

The sailors made to help Mary, but once again she was apprehensive of physical contact. Of course in their eagerness to help Gary and Rommel were continually trying to drag her along at too fast a pace. With great difficulty we worked out a method whereby she could lean on Gary and Rommel without their exerting any pressure. Once sitting at the Bar Mary ordered a brandy which Philippa served. The Captain arrived and bowed.

Mary said 'Thank you for saving my life', and everyone said 'Cheers'. Rommel pressed a button which finally shut the Bow Doors and the scene ended.

 TEA BREAK

After tea we ran through the scene once more, side coaching all action and dialogue. We then discussed the Ferry's destination. We wanted somewhere with lots of noise and people. Mary said she wanted to go *shopping*.

Benny began to dance a jig and make bagpipe noises. Where do bagpipes come from? '*Edinburgh*'. We brainstormed shop ideas, and then did quickfire mimes of our purchases:

- hat
- music
- dress
- café
- shoes
- camera

We made a note of these ideas for next time.

In the interim we went to Philippa's client review. She made it clear that she wanted to continue coming to 'drama' and that she liked everyone in the class. The following guidelines were laid down for responding to disruptive behaviour.

1.   As soon as she starts screaming tell her no, if the noise continues Philippa must leave the session.

2.   If she continues to scream and is disturbing the rest of the college then she has to go outside and calm down. When calm she can come inside again.

SESSION FOUR

We rehearsed Scene One *The Ferry*. This time Tom, and David who had been absent, combined to make the Bow Doors. Everyone else remembered their roles very well, and we could concentrate on issues such as projection and masking each other. Gary and Graham found concentration most difficult. They knew each other well and were constantly giggling and looking to each other for approval. Both of them were actually very capable, but, like many actors, needed constant reassurance. Their habit was to say 'I can't do it' when the going got tough, but by constant praise and refocusing they did succeed in concentrating through the scene. Gary enjoyed his role of upright sailor, enjoyed saluting and being the leader out of the two sailors. Responsibility was obviously not something he was used to, and he responded well. Graham obviously found working closely with Mary, a much older woman, quite intimidating. He would often look to his friends Gary and Rommel, for support instead of staying in role as Mary's partner. Over the weeks, though, he became more confident and was able to respond to her.

Scene Two: Princes Street

We spent a lot of time working out who would be in charge of which shop.

- Benny immediately mimed some headphones and became the music shop.

- David has a large wardrobe of hats so he became the Hat Seller.

- Tom instantly became a very vocal sales assistant, producing a coat for Mary to try on, so his became the Clothes Shop.

- Rommel is very proud of his shoes and his ability to take them off and put them on, so he became the Shoe Shopkeeper.

- Philippa, in her chair was already conveniently placed to be at a café table, and Gary loves to be helpful, so he became a Waiter. They decided it would be an Italian restaurant serving spaghetti.

- Kwouk Seng couldn't give us a suggestion, so we decided to wait to see what was needed before giving him a shop.

We thought about the positioning of the shops. Should they be on both sides of the road? No, only one side so that the audience could see the Honeymoon Couple going into each one.

We set up an improvisation whereby people could explore being in their individual shops. On 'Action' they had to serve someone and try not to let them leave the shop without buying.

Tom produced a lovely mirror and was very flattering to his customers. David took his hat off and on and offered to sell it to anyone. Rommel squatted down on the floor and took off his shoe. When he invited Mary to sit down and try on shoes he was very anxious to help Mary take hers off too, for realism. Mary was adamant she didn't want anyone to touch her shoes – reluctant once more to try physical contact. Rommel was persuaded to mime the action.

TEA BREAK

Once most people had established their routines inside their shops Mary and Graham began a tour of them. Each time the couple would look inside and were asked 'Would you like to try something?' Mary decided each time whether to say Yes or No. At the Clothes Shop she tried on a coat, looked at herself in the mirror, asked Graham if he liked it and decided to buy it. Graham produced the money, Tom rang it up and gave change. This was by far the most complicated exchange.

At the Shoe Shop she was invited to sit down and try on a pair of shoes, which Rommel put on for her. She declined to buy them.

At the Café the couple looked at the diners eating spaghetti and decided to walk on by.

At the Music Shop they both tried on Benny's headphones, danced a little to the music and walked out.

At the last shop, Kwouk's, we asked Mary what she would like to buy. She said a camera, so Kwouk became the Camera Seller, miming taking a picture.

This led to the final tableau of the couple reaching the end of Princes Street, turning, taking a picture of all the shops who 'froze' in characteristic poses to end the scene.

This week Philippa came with a new carer, Roslyn, a very dynamic woman who was full of energy and ideas for both her work with Phil and the work in drama. This made all the difference to Phil's enjoyment and consequently her behaviour in college. It was really wonderful to see the change this new relationship brought to her.

SESSION FIVE

We went back to the original ideas for holiday destinations. Where could the couple visit next? Everyone loved going to the Beach and also some people had fixed ideas about beach scenes from soap series. Elements of this crept into the final scene!

- Mary settled herself under a tree to read in the shade.
- Graham produced some binoculars and gazed out to sea.
- Gary threw himself enthusiastically on to the ground and began to swim.
- Philippa mimed eating an ice cream.
- David sat on a chair positioned in the sea, which then became a pedalo.
- Rommel sat on a stool and painted a picture of David.
- Kwouk, lying down beside Mary, was persuaded to apply sun-tan cream to his arms.
- Benny leapt into the sea and became a shark.

The first improvisation with these characters led inexorably to the shark attacking everyone on the beach, and general mayhem! We examined what had happened, and identified the various elements of the scene. For the second improvisation the shark only attacked the swimmer. David, on the pedalo, was very brave and beat the monster with an oar while calling for help. Graham, on shore, saw what was happening through his binoculars, stood up and called for lifeguards. Everyone began shouting encouragement to the swimmer and his saviour. When they reached shore everyone clapped and the shark swam away.

We had to repeat this scene several times to establish the sequence of events, and persuade the shark not to eat the swimmer! It turned out to be an excellent scene for focusing the whole cast's attention on the somewhat melodramatic action. Each person had their own individual task or moment and they were all responsible for the attitude to the rescue.

Rehearsing this scene took most of the session – refining the small amount of dialogue and establishing the sequence of events.

We went back and rehearsed all three scenes so far.

At the end of the session we talked about the next scene and decided that the next venue should be Disneyland or a funfair. We joined hands in a circle and improvised the communal noises of pleasure and anticipation everyone makes on 'white knuckle rides'. We concentrated on using diaphragms to push out big sounds and on opening our mouths as wide as possible in our excitement and fear.

We started on a low or quiet note with everyone's heads in the centre looking at the floor, and for the louder notes, we threw heads back, and our arms above our head. The group was asked to think about different rides for next time.

SESSION SIX

We rehearsed the beach scene first.

The session concentrated on *fairground rides* and *sounds*.

The *Ghost Train* was something everyone had experienced, and was a good ride because it used everyone at the same time while also spotlighting individuals. The students stood in a semicircle, facing the audience. One by one each person got into a train carriage, holding on to a rail in front and moved past the others slowly. The method of progress varied. Some pretended they were indeed in a train and shuffled rhythmically, making train sounds, while others just walked, and some had to be coaxed. Each waiting person became a ghost train surprise and made faces or eerie noises to make the traveller jump. There were skeletons, spider webs and bats flying in faces. For some travellers this was quite frightening, for others, hilarious. Some wanted to stop and be frightening in return, others hid their faces. We stopped and divided the group into two. Half became monsters and half responded to the monsters. We asked the monsters to tower over their victims and the victims to react. Would they shrink and become smaller, would they run away would they hide their heads in their hands, would they laugh or would they ignore it? Eventually by practising in pairs and all together everyone got the idea and it became a completely enjoyable and more controlled experience.

The *Ghost Train* worked in this way. The person at the downstage left edge of the semicircle began by getting in the train and moving round the inside edge, encountering the surprises. When s/he reached the end of the line everyone took two paces to the left to reform the shape and then the next person began their journey.

Montezuma's Revenge was a roller-coaster ride inspired by the noises we had discovered last time. Everyone sat in a line on the edge of the stage facing the audience with their legs dangling over the edge. They sat close together with arms linked. We had to be careful about positioning people and take into consideration concentration levels and also weight, so there was no danger of anyone being inadvertently pulled or crushed. The simple idea was for everyone to lean forward making an 'oooo' sound and then back with an 'aaaah' sound, swinging legs high as they leant back to lean on the stage. At first, co-ordinating the line required counting in and conducting forward and back. We had to continually impress on people the necessity of working as a team, following the conductor because of the danger of arms being pulled and backs being strained as people moved at different times. Eventually it became a smooth ride.

The Black Hole was another roller-coaster. It represented an important development for Philippa as it was the first time she had ever wanted to get out of her chair in class and on to the floor. Everyone sat on the floor in a line one behind the other with legs stretched either side of the person in front. Philippa as the smallest, was at the front with Roslyn. Tom and Kwouk were at the back, being the largest. Again, following a conductor, everyone leant right forward with an 'oooo' sound and then backwards lifting arms high in the air with an excited 'eeee' sound. There was a great sense of movement, team excitement, and togetherness each time we did this.

The *Performance* went off remarkably smoothly. After the audience had gone we had a debriefing with the cast about how they had felt. We were extremely pleased at the level of concentration. The stimulus of the audience had made Tom and Benny improvise more lines in their roles, in character and with a degree of vocal power we had not heard previously from either of them. Mary and Graham had stayed together in the Ferry and Shopping scenes, which had been a problem and had been aware of their stage positions in the shops very well, so for once we were able to see and hear exactly what was happening. Philippa had needed no reminding to serve the drinks in the Bar, and had amazed everyone with her dexterity on the floor in The Black Hole.   Kwouk Seng's greatest personal achievement was in taking control of his Car and creating a brake, door and window. In the end he didn't even have to follow anyone on to the ship. David had shown great authority in his role as saviour on the beach. We felt that without exception everyone had grown in confidence. Everyone was elated. We finished the term with a party!

PART IV

Working with People with Multiple and Profound Disabilities

BEA CH BEACH

Working with People with Multiple and Profound Disabilities

Day Centres and Further Education Colleges offering drama courses for people with Special Needs usually differ in their student make up. In most you will find mixed ability groups – students varying in their extent of disability. Generally it is quite possible to find a middle ground of working which accommodates both ends of the scale of people's needs and abilities.

Some groups of students will contain maybe a few individuals in wheelchairs, and it is important to adapt the games and exercises to include them. Occasionally there will be one or two students who have more profound and multiple disabilities and it is usual for those individuals to be supported by individual carers or support workers. In this case your work should reflect the capabilities and needs of the majority, with the supported workers concentrating on their own students – adapting or making sure that they feel included.

Other students are often eager to help and work with their more profoundly disabled contemporaries, sometimes to the point of over-anxiousness – pushing the chair when not appropriate, too much touch, etc. You will need to be extra sensitive and diplomatic when dealing with such situations. Such integration is very positive for the profoundly disabled students. They enjoy the stimulation and companionship of working with other people, of being brought to a new environment, and being encouraged to express themselves in any way that they can.

If you are working with a group made up entirely of students with multiple and profound disabilities you will need to change the thrust of your work. Rather than plan for a workshop which is about doing and taking part, you need to devise sessions which are stimulatory and about having things done to you – more about receiving than doing.

We have found the most successful way of working with such groups is to plan workshops which are all about sensory perception and awareness. The five senses need to be stimulated: *hearing, sight, smell, touch* and *taste*. To relate this to drama, you could incorporate this sense stimulation into a narrative story in which the students get involved, or are taken on a sensory journey of some description.

You will need to think carefully about the length of your session. If people have profound physical disabilities, in general it will take longer to assemble everyone in one place. Think about how the space affects the session. You will probably want to create a comfortable environment which could possibly involve lying on mats and bean bags. If students are to be transferred out of their chairs you will need to consider the involvement of lifting equipment, hoists, etc. Insist that each student is accompanied by a support worker who can cater for their individual needs should any situations arise which you are not trained to deal with.

Before embarking on your sense stimulation session make sure you check with support workers if students have any particular *allergies* to substances you may be about to use. Often people with more profound and multiple disabilities have more complicated hypoallergenic reactions than others.

Probably about half an hour is a good length for the body of work in the session as you have to bear in mind attention spans and that these students will tire more easily than others.

UNDER THE SEA

This is an example of a theme we have used in the past with groups of students with profound and multiple disabilities.

Students were lowered onto mats and supportive bean bags, with floor area covered with a mixture of blue chiffon type material and bubble wrap.

Pre recorded *music* and *sound effects*: sea noises – 'Calmer Panorama', dolphins, whales, etc.

Other sounds the story contained offered opportunities for the students to contribute vocally – the noise of the sea, waves, weather, etc. –

and also contributing non-verbally by banging the floor and clapping, being given different objects to hit or shake.

Decoration: we created lines across the space using string or rope, to hang brightly coloured fish shapes, starfish, silver wigs which looked like anemones or squid – we had had these previously made in a session at the same centre with a different group. When hanging things or placing objects around the room, make sure that these will be within the students eyeline.

We created *movement* of the sea with streamers of coloured materials that were passed over heads and hands. We provided different feeling materials, for example, silk, fur, linen, sacking, chiffon, netting, thick and thin ropes.

Objects: things we used included a 'treasure chest' – a box containing objects like coins to plunge hands into as it passed round via carers. Also used was a bucket containing seaweed or simulated seaweed – grass, foliage, spaghetti in water, etc. A box of sand is always useful for people to run their hands through and feel different textures, heats, etc.

Smell: the smelling of the bucket of salty, briny water. We also sprayed fine water mist above students' heads and onto hands. It can be a good idea to put a smell into the water using natural oils, for example, aromatherapy oils, even having some burning constantly from the side.

We cannot stress too heavily how important it is prior to the session to check out if participants have any allergies and how their supporters usually work with their students.

If you have access to *lighting* you can achieve some great effects with different coloured gels, colour wheels and lighting effects called *gobos* which make patterns across a space. Where there is no sophisticated lighting, experiment with some coloured gels and torches – most colleges and Day Centres will have access to an overhead projector which can be used to creative effect.

If no 'effect' lighting can be found, you could simply begin the session with the blinds nearly drawn, or with the lights very low and gradually make the space lighter by opening curtains, etc. – this will at least provide some sort of change in atmosphere.

Narrative: *tell a story*. If you are using a sea theme, spin a tale of life under sea, or a journey or adventure that involves much *movement*, for example, 'and the sea becomes rougher' – students can be helped to move by their support workers. A phrase such as 'all the sailors were surrounded by a school of tiny fish who nibbled at hands and feet' could employ support workers to lightly tap or squeeze on hands and feet with their fingertips.

Include passages where people can get together in pairs where possible – either moments of *interaction* between student and carer or in fours, i.e. two students and two carers. Encourage touching and vocal communication. Also a passage when everyone touches/holds hands – encourage feeling of community.

Try and create physical *events* in the story – storms where you can use the lights, movement and noises, etc. *Pace* the story to include crescendos and moments of calm – probably end with a very calm relaxing passage to include stroking, etc.

In a weekly session with children of five years of age who had profound and multiple disabilities we took them on a journey on a 'ship' each week. The sessions were structured so that a different adventure occurred: we found a desert island with tropical fruit; we used passion fruit and mangoes to feed to people. We would act as the captain and first mate. Everyone was 'piped' and welcomed aboard – we made the ship shape with pieces of ribbon around their mats and chairs, and saluted them off to 'land' at the end of the session.

Companies which specialise in working with people with profound and multiple disabilities whose work we know of and highly recommend are *Entelechy* – who run workshops and residencies – and *Oily Cart* (tel: 0208 672 6329) – a London based theatre company who tour mainly to special schools offering a stimulating participatory play/workshop in a specially made sensory environment run by several professional actors.

PART V

Touring Survival Guide

Bus

BUS

Sophie Specker

Touring Survival Guide

NOTES ON WORKING AWAY FROM YOUR USUAL SPACE
Call Sheets

If you are taking a group of people on tour, if only for a day-trip, make sure you give them, or send to their home well in advance, a call sheet (letter) clearly outlining the arrangements. Include:

- Address/contact phone number of performance venue/digs (if staying overnight).
- Date/time/place of pick up.
- Approximate time of return to base.
- Arrangements for travel to own homes if necessary. (Try to avoid being solely responsible for individual drop offs, particularly late at night – it can be exhausting!)
- What to wear.
- Meal arrangements.
- Money – will any be needed? If so, approximately how much?

Refreshments

Avoid unnecessary anxiety by clearly stating the timetable for meal breaks. Having lunch at an unfamiliar time has been known to cause stress, so make sure everyone knows what time meals are, and who is providing them. On a day-trip it's most practical to ask everyone to bring their own packed lunch or tea.

Restaurants

Set your budget. Your organisation will only have limited funds for meal expenses. Therefore it's only reasonable to tell your group to order from a limited selection of items. Even if people are using their own money they may well need guidance in ordering. If there are two of you leading the group of ten, say, sit down individually with the two tables of five and discuss the menu before the waiter arrives. This not only saves time, but it also means that you will know what's been ordered in case individuals have forgotten by the time the food arrives. If possible, be aware of individual's eating patterns. You may find, for example that someone is prone to ordering too much, and then feeling/being sick later in the minibus or before they go on stage. Be ready with advice!

Purchase a *guide* to pubs or restaurants – it can be invaluable to book somewhere pleasant in advance.

Medication

If you are travelling with someone on regular medication, make sure you are aware of its name and dosage. It is inadvisable to travel with anyone who is not capable of regulating their own drugs.

Periods

It can be useful to travel with a small supply of sanitary protection. Also to be aware of individual women's usual methods of coping with period discomfort.

First Aid

A first aid pack should be travelled and it would be extremely useful if any accompanying carers had completed a first aid course.

In the Theatre/Performance Space

Try to arrive in *good time*. The company should have time to explore the unfamiliar acting area, relax, and possibly have a meal before the show. (Although we'd advise having the meal at least an hour before any performance.)

Dressing Rooms. Somewhere should be designated as a changing facility, with access to toilets. It's preferable to have a room for each sex, though unfortunately not always available, even in a professional space.

Warm-up. Leave yourself enough time to do a company warm-up half an hour before the show. Twenty minutes, incorporating vocal and movement work and possibly a small section of the show should be about right. A quick and effective individual exercise is for everyone to say a short line from the show, filling the new space with the sound of their voice, and for everyone else to repeat it loudly too. Obviously if it's a 'one-off' performance it would be a good thing to do a run through before the audience arrives.

Tiredness

Try to avoid it! Emphasise the need for a good night's sleep before the performance, and try to ensure a rest before the actual show. Energy levels can very quickly drop, and nerves sometimes don't emerge to carry people through.

Accommodation

To be arranged strictly according to budget of course. Find out in advance if possible whether people of the same sex are comfortable with sharing rooms. Some people may actually prefer it, and again some people may benefit from help dressing or undressing. On the other hand there may be disagreements between those who like to sleep with a light on, or those that like to watch TV until late and those who don't. It is advisable to have *ensuite* rooms, as the locking of shared bathroom doors can be forgotten, or lead to problems with unlocking.

Entertainment

If you are away for a few days you may find a moment to have some fun! The *cinema* is always a popular, and not tiring way to fill an afternoon. The difficulty as with every large group is in finding a film to suit every taste. Looming large in our legend is the time we took a group to see *Babe* which appealed to 9 of the 10 of us. However the one dissenter made our lives hell for several hours afterwards with one of the most major sulks ever recorded! Be aware that most cinemas do a discount in the afternoon, and may do a special deal for a disabled party. *Other attractions* do special prices, and sometimes, free entry for carers. *A drink after the show* is a good way to unwind and gives people the opportunity to order for themselves and spend their own money.

Free Time

Everyone should have some. It is unreasonable for everyone to spend the whole day in each other's pockets. Depending on the make-up of your group you may be able to allow people to explore a new town, for example, in groups of threes, naming a return time and venue. Or it may be a good idea to suggest some private time during the day for resting in the hotel room. And don't forget yourselves – you need a break too.

List of Exercises/Games

PART 1
SESSION 1: GETTING TO KNOW YOU

1. Bathtime for Barbara
2. Alphabet Queue
3. Body Words
4. Name that Ball
5. Getting to Know You
6. Making a Machine
7. Relaxation Journey

SESSION 2: COMMUNICATION

1. Presenting Self with Action
2. Hello My Name is…
3. Circle One Word Association
4. Giant Gestures
5. Knives and Forks
6. Do You Like Your Neighbour?
7. Zip, Zap, Boing

SESSION 3: EYE CONTACT

1. Hello, How are You?
2. The Eye of the Circle
3. Is there Something in my Eye?
4. Friends Across the Sea
5. Band Leader

6.   Mirror Pairs
7.   Monster Murder

SESSION 4: CONCENTRATION

1.   Keeper of the Keys
2.   Crossing the River
3.   What are you Doing? Or Liar!
4.   Grandmother's Footsteps
5.   Numbers into a Circle
6.   Newspaper Islands and Sharks

SESSION 5: LISTENING

1.   Sounds in the Room
2.   Atmospherics
3.   Soundtrack Story
4.   Chinese Whispers
5.   One Word Story
6.   Where are You, Adam?
7.   Alpine Calls
8.   Captain's Coming

SESSION 6: TRUST

1.   Back to Back and Up and Down
2.   Blindfold Walk
3.   Trust Circle
4.   Dancing in the Dark
5.   Tangle and Untangle

SESSION 7: MEMORY

1. Kim's Game
2. My Grandmother Went to Market
3. Clothes basket or The Magic Box
4. Grandmother's Story
5. Appealing for Witnesses
6. Detective
7. Farmer, Pig, Wolf

SESSION 8 – FEELINGS

1. Response Sculpture 1
2. Hugging and Stroking
3. Response Sculpture 2
4. The Oh Game
5. Emotional Statues
6. Emotional Photographs

SESSION 9: SOUNDS AND RHYTHM

1. Spiral Sounds
2. Sound Symphony
3. Name Rhythm
4. Cookie Jar
5. Eurovision Song Contest

SESSION 10: BASIC IMPROVISATION

1. Presents
2. 'I'm Sorry I Broke your....'
3. Ironing Board and Horses!
4. Commercial Break
5. Accept and Build
6. Send a Letter

PART 2
SESSION 11: INTRODUCING OR FINDING A THEME

1. Fruit Salad or Physical Warm-Up
2. Ideas Session
3. Brainstorming
4. Soap Opera
5. Tackling the Themes

SESSION 12: BUILDING CONFIDENCE AND PRESENTATION

1. Presentation of Self to Group as Audience
2. Scenes
3. Storyboarding
4. The Way Ahead

SESSION 13: PROGRESSING FROM MOVEMENT TO DANCE

1. Only Connect
2. Name Dance
3. Holidays
4. Romeo and Juliet

SESSION 14: DISCOVERING YOUR VOICE

1. Tribal Chant
2. Tribal Challenge
3. Wishing Well
4. Basic Alexander Technique and Relaxation
5. Find Your Centre/Address the Audience
6. Open Vowels
7. Breath Control
8. Nasality

SESSION 15: STATUS AND MIME

1. Master/Servant
2. High and Low
3. Door-to-Door Selling
4. Swapping Status Mid-Way
5. Job Interviews
6. Romeo and Juliet Status
7. Holiday Status

SESSION 16: STYLE

1. Film Night
2. Video Night
3. Whose Line is it Anyway?
4. Tea Time
5. Swordfighting
6. Adverts Anonymous
7. Working Towards Performance
8. Box of Tricks
9. Four Scenes

SESSION 17: BUILDING A CHARACTER

1. Shortcut Characters
2. Funny Walks
3. Mannerisms on a Bus
4. Voices and Accents in a Pub
5. Cinema Queue
6. Hot Seating
7. Coping with the Media
8. Physicality
9. Design a Costume
10. Performance Theme: Brainstorming

SESSION 18: USING THE RIGHT WORDS

1. Theatre Personnel
2. The Theatre or the House
3. Inside the Auditorium
4. On-Stage
5. Working on-Stage
6. Backstage
7. Calls
8. Rehearsals
9. Lighting
10. Props
11. Scenery
12. Curtains

SESSION 19: RECORDING AND LISTENING TO YOUR VOICE

Developing your voice

1. Microphone Circle
2. Guess the Voice
3. Confidence and Clarity
4. Accents and Finding a Voice
5. Chords
6. Mike-Stand Presenting/PA
7. Recording Songs
8. Walkmans
9. Using the Technology
10. Interviewing on Tape
11. Sampler Boards

Creating An Artistic End Product

1. Six-Minute Scene
2. Soap Opera
3. News Bulletin
4. Radio Commercials
5. Creation of a Soundtrack
6. Looking at Music
7. Desert Island Discs
8. Disc Jockeys

SESSION 20: VIDEOING AND WATCHING YOURSELF

1. Video Equipment
2. Visual Record
3. Filming
4. Teaching Tool
5. Taster Days

Bibliography

Bailey, S.D. (1993) *Wings to Fly – Bringing Theatre Arts to Students with Special Needs*. Rockville, USA: Woodbine House.

Cameron, J. (1995) *The Artist's Way – A Spiritual Guide to Higher Creativity*. London: Pan Books.

Jennings, S. (1986) *Creative Drama in Groupwork*. Bicester: Winslow Press.

Johnstone, K. (1981) *IMPRO: Improvisation and the Theatre*. London: Methuen.

Rawlins, G. and Rich, J. (1992) *Look Listen and Trust – A Framework for Learning throuh Drama*. Walton-on-Thames: Nelson.

Schtzman, M. and Cohen-Cruz, J. (eds) (1994) *Playing Boal – Theatre, Therapy, Activism*. London: Routledge.